JAPANESE KOSHER COOKING

Sushi, Sushi and More

JAPANESE KOSHER COOKING

Sushi, Sushi and More
With Ingredients In Your Refrigerator

KINUE WEINSTEIN

Photography by
Kinue Weinstein

KTAV Publishing House, Inc.
Jersey City, NJ

Library of Congress Cataloging-in-Publication Data

Imai-Vinshtain, Kinu'eh, 1948-
  Japanese kosher cooking : sushi, sushi and more with ingredients in
your refrigerator / Kinue Weinstein.
      p. cm.
  ISBN-13: 978-0-88125-957-5
  1. Cookery, Japanese. 2. Cookery, Jewish. I. Title.
  TX724.5.J3W44 2007
  641.5952--dc22

                                                        2007020007

                    Printed in Hong Kong

                         Published by
              KTAV Publishing House, Inc.
                    930 Newark Avenue
                  Jersey City, NJ 07306
                 Email: bernie@ktav.com
                       www.ktav.com
                     (201) 963-9524
                   Fax (201) 963-0102

CONTENTS

3. SALADS AND PICKLES 29

4. FISH 43

5. MEAT, POULTRY, AND EGGS 59

6. TABLE COOKING *101*

7. VEGETABLES *123*

★Indicates recipes that are vegetarian or that make good vegetarian dishes by eliminating meat or fish and by replacing chicken or fish soup stock with water.

APPENDIX *193*

PREFACE

Making Japanese food kosher is easier than you think. When I lived in Jerusalem in the 1970s, my friend Mariko Tsujita and I wrote a Far Eastern cookbook based on ingredients available in Israel. In those days, there were no sushi restaurants or Japanese food markets. When we couldn't find Japanese foods, my friend and I adapted or substituted local ingredients to simulate Japanese cooking. For example, we substituted turkey for pork, carrots for bamboo shoots, and sherry and sugar for *mirin* (Japanese cooking wine). Our reliance on local ingredients made it easy to observe the rules of kashruth, and in Japan, as in China and Korea, there isn't much dairy in the cuisine. Our recipes appeared in *The Far Eastern Cookbook*, which was published in Hebrew by Edanim in 1980.

Here in the United States, where I have lived since 1980, there are many Japanese food stores in the large cities and an abundance of ingredients imported from Japan. However, the nearest Japanese supermarket to the New Jersey suburb where I live is 45 minutes away. Accordingly, I have been improvising Japanese cooking with ingredients that are available from near-by supermarkets. Quite often, as a matter of convenience, I find myself using the same recipes I used in Israel. As a result, I have realized that my friends who keep kosher kitchens can cook perfectly kosher Japanese, Chinese, and Korean dishes without special ingredients and the extra expense. So don't be discouraged by the fact that there aren't many kosher items directly imported from the Far East at the local Oriental food market. All you need to cook kosher Oriental meals is kosher soy sauce, which is readily available. I am delighted to see many more kosher Japanese ingredients available in the United States today than in Israel in the 1970s, such as tofu (soybean curd), miso (soybean paste), nori (seaweed), *wakame, kombu, hiziki* (all dried sea-vegetables), agar, *soba* (buckwheat pasta), *udon* (wheat-and-rice pasta), and even *mirin* (rice wine for cooking). They are available in the kosher section of supermarkets and at kosher healthfood stores, and they are distributed by American companies, such as Eden Foods. The ingredients are just as good as those in Japan, particularly the *umeboshi* (pickled *ume* plum).

I have decided to share my Japanese recipes to help the busy men and women who keep kosher. These recipes are easy to make at home in your kosher kitchen: Japanese cooking, Chinese-style cooking, and Korean-style cooking, all using ingredients available at your local supermarket. I've also changed my old recipes and added new ones more in sync with our health-conscious culture. In addition, I have indicated when you can use the original Japanese ingredients, should you have the opportunity to obtain them.

These recipes will add exotic variety to your dinner table. If you wish to create a touch of an Oriental atmosphere to go along with the menu, there are a number of changes that you might make in your dining style. For instance, you can use Japanese utensils and serving dishes. You can also try do-it-yourself table cooking, such as sukiyaki, on your dining-room table. Chopsticks and small pottery dishes with sauce and pickles also add authenticity to the table. Or you can prepare several main dishes of Chinese-style Japanese cooking and place them in the center of the table or on a lazy Susan so that guests can help themselves.

The recipes in this book can be put to a variety of uses, ranging from a simple lunch to a multi-course dinner. By controlling the portions, many of the recipes can be used as main dishes, appetizers, or snacks. Some of the recipes can be combined with Western dishes. Vegetarians who are looking for diversity in their diet will find a number of suitable dishes. Aside from dishes made only of vegetables, I have indicated those from which the meat may be easily eliminated. What you do with these recipes remains up to you. You are free to innovate! However you decide to use them, I hope that you will enjoy these new additions to your repertoire.

I am not a culinary professional—just a busy woman with a full-time job and a family who likes my cooking. I gained cooking experience by making dinner for my two children and my husband almost every single day for decades. I always ate dinner with my children until they left for college. Aside from the fact that I feel strongly that it is important to eat dinner together with one's children, discussing the day's events, it was a tremendous pleasure for me to watch them eat my cooking. I thank my son Daniel, my daughter Naomi, and my husband Steve, who gave me such pleasure cooking for them. They particularly liked Japanese food, which led me to prepare Japanese dishes with the ingredients available in my refrigerator. Without my family, I might never have learned how to cook. I also thank the friends who taught me about kashruth and shopping for kosher food: Patricia Rotbard, Tina Zegas, and Eugene Rosenthal.

1. APPETIZERS

There are no specific recipes for appetizers in Japan. Of course, many main courses may be served as appetizers by reducing the portion, including sushi, deep-fried chicken, *yakitori*, dumplings, and sashimi. Others, such as egg custard (*chawan-mushi*), chilled tofu (*hiyayakko*), and vegetable dishes, can be served during the main course or after the manner of Spanish tapas cuisine.

I have selected a sampling of dishes that could be served as appetizers.

1-1: EGG CUSTARD (CHAWAN-MUSHI)

SERVES 4

3 eggs
1½ cups chicken soup stock
¼ teaspoon salt
1 teaspoon soy sauce
½ teaspoon sugar
¼ pound chicken breast meat marinated in 1 tablespoon soy sauce
3 shiitake mushrooms (or any mushrooms) sliced
6 snow peas
8 mitsuba leaves, or 8 Italian parsley leaves

Mix the eggs, soup stock, salt, soy sauce, and sugar in a bowl.
Cut the chicken into small pieces, and put them in the bowl.

Place the mixture in 4 heat-resistant bowls small enough to fit into a steamer. Garnish each bowl with the shiitake mushrooms, snow peas, and parsley.

Put the bowls in a steamer and bring to a boil. Steam bowls over high heat for 5 minutes, then simmer for another 15 minutes. (*Do not put your hands in the steamer while steaming.*)

Serve hot with a spoon.

1-2: CHILLED TOFU (HIYAYAKKO)

SERVES 4

TOFU:
13 ounces ready-made kosher tofu

Or make your own egg tofu as follows:
4 eggs
1 cup chicken soup stock or water
¼ teaspoon salt
1 teaspoon sugar
1 tablespoon white wine

SAUCE:
½ cup chicken soup stock
1 tablespoon soy sauce

1 tablespoon grated lemon peels
4 thin slices of lemon

In a pan, boil water, and cook tofu for 4 minutes over a low fire. Chill and cut the tofu into 4 pieces. Place each piece in a small individual bowl.

Or make your own egg tofu as follows:

Add the salt, white wine, and sugar to the chicken soup stock.
Beat the eggs, and combine with the soup mixture.
Pour the egg-and-soup mixture in a square pan that will fit in your steamer. (A soufflé pan may better fit a round steamer.)
Steam the mixture 20–30 minutes over low heat.
Let cool. Keep the egg curd in your refrigerator until you serve.
Before serving, carefully remove the egg curd from the pan, using a knife to separate the egg curd from the edges of the pan, and cut it into 4 pieces.
Place each piece in a small individual bowl.

To make the sauce, mix the chicken soup stock, and soy sauce in a small pan, and bring to boil. Let cool.

Pour the sauce over the tofu or egg tofu, and serve with a garnish of lemon peels and slices.
Serve cold with a teaspoon.

Note: Egg tofu, just like regular tofu made of soybeans, can be used with many other Japanese dishes (e.g., cut into pieces and added to miso soup).

1-3: SKEWERED GRILLED CHICKEN (MINI-YAKITORI)

SERVES 4

½ pound chicken breast meat or boneless thigh meat (depending on
   your preference)
1 stalk of leek, or ½ round onion
½ green pepper

MARINADE:
1 tablespoon sugar
1½ tablespoons soy sauce
1 tablespoon sugar★
3 tablespoons white wine★

★You can replace the sugar and white wine with 3 tablespoons kosher *mirin*.
You can also use kosher teriyaki sauce instead of the ingredients above.

Cut the chicken meat into 1½-inch cubes.

Cut the leeks into pieces 1½ inches long. (If a round onion is used, cut into 4 sections and separate each section into 2 pieces.)

Cut the green pepper into 8 sections.

Prepare 4 skewers. Fill each skewer by alternately placing chicken pieces, a piece of leek (or 1 piece of a round onion section), and 1 section of green pepper.

Combine all the ingredients for the marinade.

Grill all the skewers at the same time while basting them with the marinade at least 5 times. (If there is not enough sauce, make more using the same proportions.)

1-4: SPICY CHICKEN DRUMSTICKS (KARA-AGE)

SERVES 4

8 small chicken drumsticks, or 4 large drumsticks, cut in half

1 egg
1 teaspoon white wine
4 tablespoons cornstarch
¼ teaspoon powdered garlic
¾ teaspoon powdered chili
¾ teaspoon salt
Dash of red pepper (increase the amount if you like spicy food)

Oil for deep-frying

Remove the skin from the drumsticks.
Combine the egg, wine, cornstarch, garlic powder, chili powder, salt, and red pepper in a bowl.
Put the chicken drumsticks in the bowl, and coat them well.
Heat the oil, and drop the chicken pieces, one by one, into the oil.
Deep-fry until golden brown. Remove the chicken and drain on a paper towel.

Note: This goes well with beer, and it is a popular summer dish at rooftop beer gardens in Japan.

1-5: SPINACH WITH SESAME SAUCE

SERVES 4

8–10 ounces spinach leaves, or 1 bunch of spinach leaves (½ pound)

SAUCE:
3 tablespoons black sesame seeds (or white sesame seeds)
2 tablespoons white miso
1 tablespoon white wine
2 tablespoons honey
⅓ teaspoon salt

Boil the spinach. Drain. Let cool.
Toast sesame seeds in a frying pan and crush. (see page 193)
In a bowl, combine all the ingredients for the sauce, and mix well.
Cut the spinach into 2-inch pieces, and pour the sauce over it.

1-6: EGGPLANT SALAD

S̲ERVES 4

1 large eggplant (about 1½ pounds)

S̲AUCE:
1½ tablespoons soy sauce
2 tablespoons soup stock

O̲PTIONAL:
2 tablespoons (one handful) kosher *arame* soaked in cold water, boiled 10 minutes, and drained.

Grill the eggplant about 30 minutes.
Peel the skin while hot, and slice the eggplant meat.
Place the eggplant slices in a shallow bowl. Let cool.
Mix the ingredients for the sauce, and pour over the eggplant.
Optional: Top the dish with *arame*.

Serve cold.

1-7: FRIED EGGPLANT WITH SOYBEAN PASTE

SERVES 4

2 Italian eggplants (about 1 pound)

Oil for deep-frying

PASTE:
3 tablespoons red miso
1 tablespoon white wine or sherry
2 tablespoons honey (or sugar)
2 tablespoons soup stock

Mix all ingredients for the paste in a skillet, and bring to a boil over low heat, stirring constantly. When it becomes smooth, extinguish the flame.

Cut each of the eggplants into 4 pieces.
Heat the oil for deep-frying, and fry the 8 pieces of eggplant for a few minutes.
Top each of the 8 pieces of eggplant with the paste.

1-8: STEAMED DUMPLINGS (SHUMAI)

SERVES 4

SKIN:
1 cup flour
7 tablespoons hot water

FILLING:
6 ounces ground beef
½ round onion
¼ teaspoon ginger
¼ teaspoon salt
½ teaspoon sugar
1 tablespoon white wine or sherry
1 tablespoon sesame oil
1 tablespoon cornstarch

15 green peas

SKIN:
In a bowl, pour the hot water over the flour and mix quickly.
Cover the dough with a wet paper towel. Let stand about 30 minutes.
Divide the dough into 15 balls, and spread each ball with a rolling pin into 3-inch diameter shells on waxed paper sections.
Cover the dumpling (*shumai*) skin with a wet paper towel, and put aside.

FILLING:
Chop the onion, and combine with the rest of the filling ingredients.

Place the filling in the center of each dumpling (*shumai*) skin, and wrap from all sides, leaving an opening at the top.
Place one green pea atop each dumpling.
Place the dumplings in a steamer, and steam 10 minutes over a high flame.

Serve with mustard or soy sauce.

1-9: FRIED DUMPLINGS (GYOZA)

SKIN:
1 cup flour
7 tablespoons hot water

FILLING:
5 ounces ground beef
2 cabbage leaves
½ round onion
2 garlic cloves crushed
¼ teaspoon salt
½ teaspoon sugar
1 tablespoon white wine or sherry
1 tablespoon sesame oil
1 tablespoon cornstarch

2 tablespoons vegetable oil

⅓ cup water

DIPPING SAUCE:

4 tablespoons soy sauce
4 tablespoons vinegar
A few drops of Tabasco sauce, or a dash of red pepper

SKIN:

In a bowl, pour the hot water over the flour, and mix quickly.

Cover the dough with a wet paper towel. Let stand about 30 minutes.

Divide the dough into 15 balls, and spread each ball into a 3-inch diameter shell with a rolling pin.

Cover the skin with a wet paper towel, and set aside.

FILLING:

Chop the cabbage leaves and onion, and combine with the rest of the filling ingredients.

Place the filling in the center of each *gyoza* skin, and wrap by folding the skin and closing the top by gathering the edges.

Heat the oil in a frying pan, and place the dumplings in the frying pan, and cover. Cook over a high flame 1–2 minutes.

Pour the water into the frying pan, cover, and cook another 10 minutes over a medium flame.

Serve hot with the sauce poured into each of 4 individual dishes.

1-10: MINI-SUSHI ROLLS (HOSO-MAKI)

You'll need a sushi roller – a sheet 9 inches square made of bamboo. (see page 193)

SERVES 4

2½ cups of cooked sushi rice (see 8-1,b)
2 rectangular 8 × 7½ inch pieces of seaweed (nori) cut into half
   lengthwise pieces (see the pictures)
¼ cucumber
3 ounces imitation crabmeat

Soy sauce and wasabi mustard

Peel the cucumber, and cut thinly lengthwise.
Cut the imitation crabmeat lengthwise in the same manner.

On a sushi roller made of bamboo, place a wet paper towel (so that the seaweed won't stick to the roller).
Place a piece of seaweed on the towel.
Place rice lengthwise on the seaweed, and top with cucumber and imitation crabmeat.
Lift the sushi roller from the side closest to you and roll firmly to the other side with pressure.
Open the roller and take out the rolled sushi piece. First cut off the edges with a wet knife, and then cut the piece into 4 or 5 pieces. Keep on wetting the knife as you cut to prevent the rice from sticking to the knife.
Do the same for the remaining 3 rolls.

Serve with soy sauce and mustard.

Cut the seaweed (nori) into half lengthwise pieces.

Top with cucumber and imitation crab meat.

Lift the sushi roller.

Roll firmly.

Cut off the edges.

1-11: LOX AND AVOCADO SALAD

Serves 4

½ pound smoked salmon
2 ripe avocados
1 tomato
½ purple onion

½ lemon
1–2 lettuce leaves

Cut the smoked salmon into 1-inch pieces.
Peel the avocados and cut into ½-inch cubes.
Cut the tomato into ½-inch cubes.
Slice the onion thinly.

In a bowl, mix the salmon, avocado cubes, tomato cubes, and onion slices.
Place the lettuce leaves on 4 individual plates or shallow bowls, and place the mixture on top of the lettuce.
Cut the lemon, and serve with the salad.

2. SOUP

There are two main varieties of soup in Japan—soybean-paste (*miso*) soup and clear soup.

Soybean paste is a basic accompaniment to every meal. A typical Japanese breakfast, for instance, includes soybean-paste soup, rice, seaweed, pickles, and an egg. Many kinds of soybean paste are used; some are red and salty, others are white and sweet, sometimes the two kinds are combined. White miso and red miso are both available kosher. Because its ingredients are a good source of protein, soybean-paste soup is a nutritious dish.

Clear soup, for the most part, is served at formal meals. A small amount (about 1 cup) of clear soup is served as an appetizer. An even smaller amount of soup is sometimes served in the middle of a multi-course meal to refresh the palate.

In Japan, soup is served in a small bowl of lacquerware, and the liquid is sipped directly from the brim of the bowl. Drinking soup in this style has its own etiquette. The bowl is first picked up from the sides with both hands in the correct posture, while holding chopsticks with one hand. To pick up food from the soup with the chopsticks, the bowl is supported by one hand with the thumb on the brim and the other fingers underneath the bowl. When sipping the soup, both hands must be holding the bowl.

The soup stock can be made from a seaweed called *kombu*, dried bonito fillet, or dried young sardines. *Kombu* is available at kosher stores and is considered a health food. Clear soup made from chicken stock is quite popular in Japan. Chicken soup stock is often used for other cooking as well.

As can be seen in the following recipes, carrots and celery are not used to make chicken soup stock, unlike Western chicken soup, for the color from the vegetables spoils the clearness of the soup. Japanese soup stock, in keeping with the emphasis on natural taste and pure water, is lightly seasoned.

2-1: SOUP STOCKS

a. Chicken soup stock for clear soup
   Makes about 9 cups of soup stock

12 cups water
Whole chicken breast with bones cut into half (about 1.8–2 pounds)
1 leek or 1 round onion

Trim fat from the chicken breast.
In a large pot, pour 12 cups of water, and add the chicken meat.
Without a cover, bring to a boil and cook over a low flame for about 1 hour.

Take out the chicken and onion.
(Remove the chicken meat from the bones to use for other cooking.)

Note: If you cover the pot or cook over a high flame, the soup will not be clear.

b. Kombu stoup stock for miso soup and stews

4 cups water
1 strip (7 inches) kombu

Immerse the *kombu* in water in a pan, cover the pan and bring to a boil.
Reduce the flame, and cook for 4 minutes over a low flame.
Remove the *kombu*, and the soup stock is ready to use.

c. Fish soup stock for fish soup

5 cups water
1 head of red snapper (or any ocean fish of the same size)

Wash the red snapper head by pouring boiling water over it.

Pour 5 cups of water into a pot and put in the fish head.
Bring to a boil uncovered and cook over low heat for 15 minutes.
Pour the soup through a sieve to eliminate the fish bones.

2-2: BASIC SOYBEAN PASTE (MISO) SOUP

Serves 4

3 cups kombu soup stock (or water) (see 2-1,b)
3 tablespoons sweet white kosher miso (11% salt content)
3 stalks of green onion
6 ounces tofu or homemade egg tofu (see 1-2)

Cut the green onion into ¼-inch pieces.
Cut the tofu into 1 × ½ × ½-inch pieces.
In a pan, bring the soup stock or water to a boil.
Add the miso, and stir well. Add the onion and tofu into the soup.
Cook over a medium flame for only a few minutes.

Variations:
Instead of green onion and tofu, you can use ½ round onion and ½ potato. Cut the ½ onion into 4 pieces, and slice the potato. Cook about 5 minutes, instead of a few minutes—until the potato pieces are done.

Sliced eggplant also makes good miso soup. You can use any vegetable you wish.

2-3: SOYBEAN PASTE (MISO) SOUP WITH SEAWEED (WAKAME) AND TOFU

SERVES 4

3 cups kombu soup stock (or water) (see 2-1,b)
3 tablespoons sweet white kosher miso (11% salt content)
4 strips (7 inches each) wakame seaweed
6 ounces tofu or homemade egg tofu (see 1-2)

Soak the *wakame* strips in warm water for 15 minutes. Cut into bite-size pieces.
Cut the tofu into 1 × ½ × ¼-inch pieces.
In a pan, bring the soup stock or water to a boil.
Add the miso and *wakame*, and stir well. Add the tofu to the soup.
Cook for a few minutes over a medium flame. *Do not overcook.*

Note: *Wakame* grows in the clean, cool waters around Hokkaido and is considered a health food. *Wakame* is available at kosher food stores.

2-4: CLEAR SOUP (SUMASHI-JIRU)

SERVES 4

3 cups chicken soup stock (see 2-1,a)
½ teaspoon salt
½ teaspoon soy sauce

3 ounces boiled chicken breast meat used to make chicken soup stock
  (see 2-1,a)
4 shiitake mushrooms (or a portobello mushroom cap cut in quarters)
2 sprigs of Italian parsley

Add the salt and soy sauce to the chicken soup stock, and boil.
Slice the shiitake mushrooms thinly.
Add the chicken and shiitake mushrooms; lower the heat, and cook for 5 minutes.
Remove from heat and add the parsley leaves.

2-5: EGG SOUP

SERVES 4

4 cups soup stock
½ teaspoon salt
½ teaspoon soy sauce

4 ounces chicken breast meat used to make chicken soup stock (see 2-1,a)
2 shiitake mushrooms
½ carrot

2 slightly beaten eggs

Add the salt and soy sauce to the soup stock, and bring to a boil.

Cut the chicken into small slices.
Slice the shiitake mushrooms thinly.
Slice the carrot lengthwise into 2-inch pieces, and cut into narrow strips.
Add the chicken, sliced shiitake mushrooms, and carrot strips to the soup, and cook for 5 minutes.

Gradually pour the eggs into the soup, and remove from heat after 1 minute. *Do not overcook the eggs.*

2-6: FISH SOUP

Serves 4

4 cups fish soup stock (see 2-1,c)

½ round onion
2½ tablespoons red miso (20% salt content)
4 ounces of red snapper fillet (or any ocean white fish fillet)

In the pot, boil 4 cups of fish soup stock.
Cut the onion lengthwise into narrow slices.
Cut the fish fillet into bite-size pieces.
Add the onion and red miso to the pot, and cook for a few minutes.
Add the fish, and cook for 1–2 minutes. Remove from heat.

2-7: SALMON AND CHINESE CABBAGE SOUP

SERVES 4

4 cups fish soup stock (see 2-1,c)
1 Chinese cabbage leaf
3 tablespoons white miso (11% salt content)
1 6-ounce can of salmon

In a pot, boil 4 cups of fish soup stock.
Cut the cabbage into small pieces and add to the soup stock together with the miso. Cook for a few minutes.
Add the fish. Cook for 1–2 minutes. Remove from heat.

2-8: MIXED SOUP (KENCHIN-JIRU)

SERVES 4

½ pound white radish (daikon)
1 small carrot
2 shiitake mushrooms
2 stalks of green onion
10 ounces tofu or egg tofu (see 1-2)

2 tablespoons sesame oil

4¼ cups of chicken soup stock (see 2-1,a)
1 teaspoon salt
1 tablespoon soy sauce

Peel the white radish and carrot; slice both into bite-size pieces.
Slice the mushrooms and chop the green onions.
Cut the tofu into 1 × ½ × ¼-inch pieces.

Heat the oil in a pan and fry the white radish, carrot slices, and mushrooms.
Pour the soup and tofu pieces into the pan. Bring to a boil.
Add the salt and soy sauce.
Add the green onions, and remove from heat.

Note: You can use fish soup stock instead of chicken soup stock and add fish meat.

3. SALADS AND PICKLES

In traditional Japanese cooking, there is nothing comparable to a tossed salad. Occasionally, finely shredded raw vegetables are served with the main course, such as Japanese-style salad and shredded cabbage served with turkey schnitzel (*tonkatsu*). But *sunomono* (sliced vegetables with vinegar sauce) is popular and is served as a part of the meal.

Some of the traditional Japanese pickles, such as *takuan* (pickled white radish), use rice bran, but it is easier for Japanese to buy these pickles from the market. Several easy recipes using cucumbers are included in this chapter. The secret of good salads and pickles is using fresh vegetables.

3-1: CUCUMBER IN VINEGAR

SERVES 4

½ pound English cucumber
½ teaspoon salt
Optional: 3 7-inch strips of wakame

2 tablespoons vinegar
2 teaspoons sugar
¼ teaspoon salt
1 teaspoon soy sauce

Wash the cucumber thoroughly, without removing the skin; slice paper thin.
Add the salt, and let sit for 15 minutes.
Rinse lightly in water and drain.
Optional: Soak the *wakame* strips in a pan of warm water for 15 minutes. Bring to a boil and simmer for 5 minutes. Drain and cut into small pieces.

Combine the vinegar, sugar, salt, and soy sauce.
Just before serving, pour the sauce over the cucumber slices and mix well.
Serve chilled.

3-2: SHREDDED CABBAGE SALAD (ASAZUKE)

SERVES 4

3 cabbage leaves (8 ounces)
½ carrot
½ English cucumber (3 ounces)
1 green pepper
1 teaspoon salt

Wash the cabbage leaves.
Peel the carrot and cucumber.
Shred the cabbage leaves, carrot, cucumber, and green pepper, and place them in a bowl.
Sprinkle salt over the vegetables.
Place a plate smaller than the diameter of the bowl on top of the vegetables, and put a weight atop the plate.
Let sit for 2 hours.

Drain the water.
Serve chilled.

3-3: TOMATO SALAD

SERVES 4

2 tomatoes (½ pound)
⅓ English cucumber
½ round onion
1 tablespoon white sesame seeds

DRESSING:
4 tablespoons salad oil
2 tablespoons vinegar
¼ teaspoon salt
1 teaspoon soy sauce
dash of black pepper

Parboil the tomatoes for a few seconds, then peel.
Dice the tomatoes.
Peel the cucumber, and slice into thin rounds.
Mince the onion.

Toast the sesame seeds in a dry frying pan (without oil), and grind them well. (see page 193)
(If you do not have a grinder, wrap the sesame seeds in a cloth and crush them with a rolling pin.)

Mix the tomatoes, cucumber, onion, and sesame seeds well. Just before serving, pour the dressing over the salad.

3-4: JAPANESE SALAD

SERVES 4

3 ordinary cabbage leaves
1 carrot
3 purple cabbage leaves
1 stalk of celery
⅓ English cucumber (2 ounces)

DRESSING:

2 tablespoons soy sauce
2 tablespoons vinegar

Wash the cabbage leaves and celery.
Peel the carrot and cucumber.
Julienne the cabbage leaves, carrot, celery, and cucumber into 2-inch-long pieces.

Arrange the salad on 4 individual plates in the following order: cabbage leaves, carrot, celery, purple cabbage leaves, and cucumber.

Serve the dressing next to the platter with a spoon to pour on the salad to taste just before eating.

Sample dinner menu:
Clear soup
Japanese salad
Tempura
Rice

3-5: POTATO SALAD

2 potatoes
½ teaspoon salt
dash of black pepper

1 carrot
5 ounces frozen green peas

¼ English cucumber
½ teaspoon salt

1 teaspoon vinegar
2 tablespoons salad oil
4 tablespoons mayonnaise

Lettuce leaves

Peel the potatoes; boil them in a pot, and then mash them.
Add salt and black pepper to the potatoes while still warm.

In a pot, boil a small amount of water, and cook the carrot and peas briefly.

Peel the cucumber, slice thinly, and sprinkle with salt.

Mix the mashed potatoes and vegetables in a bowl.
Add the vinegar and salad oil to the bowl, and mix.
Add the mayonnaise, and mix well.
Serve on top of the lettuce leaves.

3-6: CUCUMBER SALAD

SERVES 4

1 English cucumber
1 clove garlic
¼ teaspoon salt
2 tablespoons soy sauce
1 tablespoon olive oil
1 tablespoon vinegar
1½ tablespoons white wine

Peel the cucumber, and cut it into thin strips 2 inches long.
Crush the garlic; combine with the remaining ingredients.
Place the shredded cucumber into a shallow bowl, and pour the sauce over the cucumber just before serving.

3-7: STRING BEANS IN SESAME SAUCE

SERVES 4

12 ounces string beans
¼ teaspoon salt

SESAME SAUCE:
3 tablespoons white sesame seeds
1 tablespoon soy sauce
1 teaspoon honey (or sugar)
1 tablespoon white wine

Wash the string beans; trim the edges, and cut in half.
In a pot, bring water to a boil, and add the string beans. Cook for 5 minutes.
Drain the beans and sprinkle them with salt.

Toast the sesame seeds in a dry frying pan (without oil), and grind them well. (see page 193)
(If you do not have a grinder, wrap the sesame seeds in a cloth and crush them with a rolling pin.)
Combine the ground sesame seeds with the rest of the sauce ingredients.
Mix the boiled string beans with the sesame sauce.

3-8: CUCUMBER AND BEAN SPROUTS SALAD

SERVES 4

½ English cucumber
½ teaspoon salt
4 ounces bean sprouts
1 small carrot

SAUCE:
1 stalk of green onion
1 clove garlic
1 hot pepper (or a dash of crushed red pepper)
1 tablespoon white sesame seeds
1 tablespoon soy sauce
1 teaspoon paprika
½ teaspoon salt

Peel the cucumbers; julienne, and sprinkle with the salt.

Wash the bean sprouts. Peel and shred the carrot. Blanch the bean sprouts and shredded carrot.

Chop the green onion, garlic, and hot pepper. Toast the sesame seeds in a frying pan (or in an oven). Mix all the ingredients for the sauce.

Squeeze the cucumber tightly to eliminate excess water. Combine the cucumber, bean sprouts, and carrot, and mix with the sauce.

Serve cold.

41

4. FISH

Fish, especially ocean fish, is best when it is fresh and in season. The sea has been a natural food reservoir for Japan, providing a variety of fish throughout the year. When I was growing up, fish was a staple of our diet. My favorite fish for a casual dinner was a simple grilled mackerel coated with salt. The rich taste of ocean fish meant that lavish seasoning was superfluous. It is common in Japan to cook the fish whole, complete with head, fins, and tail.

Sashimi, or raw fish, is probably the most famous Japanese seafood dish—and the one that foreigners find the most difficult to enjoy. Only very fresh fish, mostly coming from the ocean, can be used for sashimi. Tuna and bonito are the most common fish used for sashimi. However, salmon, yellow tail, and red snapper also may be used. They are filleted and cut into thin rectangular slices ½ inch thick, 2 inches long, and 1 inch wide. They are eaten dipped in soy sauce and wasabi mustard at the beginning of the meal with drinks.

Sashimi is kosher if the fish is kosher with scales and fins. I recommend purchasing fish for sashimi from a Japanese market, where freshness is assured due to the high turnover.

4-1: BROILED FISH

SERVES 4

4 pieces of small whole red snapper (about 1/2 pound each) or any
  ocean white fish
2 tablespoons salt

Have the fish cleaned (scales and stomach removed) at the market.
Sprinkle the salt over the fish, especially on the fins and tail just before broiling so that
the salt does not dissolve but instead crystallizes like grains of sand. (The salt is primarily decorative.)
Broil the fish 8–10 minutes per side.
Arrange the fish on dishes, setting the head to the left.

Serve hot.

In Japan, using smaller ocean fish, such as mackerel, we run two skewers through the
fish and tie the mouth shut with string before grilling. This makes the fish look as if it
were jumping out of the sea.

4-2: FRIED WHOLE FISH

SERVES 4

4 mackerels, or 4 small red snappers
Flour to cover the fish
4 shiitake mushrooms
Oil for deep-frying
1 lemon
Optional: grated white radish (daikon)
Soy sauce available at table to add to taste

Have the fish cleaned (scales and stomach removed) at the market.
Coat each fish with flour.
Deep-fry the fish.
Wash the mushrooms, and deep-fry without coating.
Serve with quartered lemons, grated white radish, and soy sauce.

4-3: BOILED FISH WITH GINGER SAUCE

SERVES 4

1 pound white fish fillet (frozen or fresh)
⅓ teaspoon salt
1 teaspoon white wine
3 tablespoons cornstarch
1 teaspoon vegetable oil

SAUCE:
⅓ teaspoon powdered ginger
2 cloves garlic
1 tablespoon vinegar
2 tablespoons soy sauce
1 tablespoon white wine
1 teaspoon sugar

GARNISH:
½ English cucumber
1 teaspoon soy sauce
1 teaspoon sugar
1 teaspoon vinegar
1 teaspoon salad oil

Dice the fish fillet into 1½-inch cubes. Season them with the salt and wine.
Coat each of the cubes with cornstarch.
Fill a pan with 4 cups of water, and bring to a boil. Put the fish cubes into the boiling water one by one. Boil for a few minutes.
Carefully remove the fish from the water with a strainer.
Pour one teaspoon of oil drop by drop over the boiled fish to prevent sticking.

Sauce:
Crush the garlic, and combine all the ingredients for the sauce.

Peel cucumber; slice thinly. Marinate the cucumber in the mixture of soy sauce, sugar, vinegar, and oil.
Arrange on a dish, setting the fish cubes in the center surrounded by the cucumber slices.

Pour the ginger sauce over the fish just before serving.
Serve hot or cold.

4-4: FISH STEAMED IN WINE

1½ pounds lemon or grey sole fish fillets
1 teaspoon salt
⅓ cup white wine

⅓ white radish (daikon)
4 green onion stems

SAUCE:
⅓ cup lemon juice
⅓ cup soy sauce

Sprinkle the fish fillets evenly with salt, and rub lightly into the fish.
Fill a steamer pot with water and bring to a boil.
Lay the fish fillets squarely in the inside pot of the steamer with no overlap.
Place the inside pot in the steamer, and pour the wine over the fish.
Steam for 10 minutes at a high flame. (*Do not put your hands in the steamer while cooking.*)

Grate the white radish (daikon), gently expressing the juice.
Mince the green onion.
Make the sauce by combining the lemon juice and soy sauce.
Arrange two or three pieces of fish on separate dishes, and ladle the green onion and white radish atop the fish.
You can also add to the sauce the liquid that issued from the fish during steaming.

Note: If your steamer is not big enough to hold all the fish at one time, steam in several batches.

4-5: SWEET AND SOUR FRIED FISH

SERVES 4

1 pound fish fillet (fresh or frozen)
1 egg
1 tablespoon cornstarch

Oil for deep-frying

1 carrot
½ green pepper
7 white mushrooms (4 ounces)
1 stalk of broccoli
½ round onion
2 tablespoons oil

SAUCE:
2 tablespoons vinegar
2 tablespoons sugar
3 tablespoons soy sauce
3 tablespoons white wine or sherry
⅓ cup water
2 tablespoons corn starch

Cube the fish fillet into bite-size pieces.
Beat the egg slightly, and add the cornstarch.
Mix with the fish cubes.
Deep-fry the fish cubes, and drain on a paper towel.

Julienne the carrot and green pepper into 2-inch pieces. Slice the onion lengthwise into thin pieces, and slice the mushrooms and broccoli. (Any other vegetables you have handy can also be used.)

Fry the vegetables in a pan in the order of carrot, green pepper, onion, broccoli, and mushrooms.

Mix all the ingredients for the sweet and sour sauce, and add it to the vegetables. Cook over a high heat until the sauce is thickened by the cornstarch.
Gently add the fried fish pieces into the vegetables and sauce so that they do not break up. Stir gently for a minute; remove from heat.

Serve hot.

4-6: GRILLED SALMON WITH SOY SAUCE

SERVES 4

1½ pounds Atlantic salmon fillet
1 lime
4 shiitake mushrooms

SAUCE:
2 tablespoons white wine
1½ teaspoons sugar
2 tablespoons soy sauce

Skin the salmon fillet, and cut it into 4 pieces.
Slice the lime thinly.
Wash the shiitake mushrooms, and cut off the stems.

Mix all the ingredients for the sauce.
Put the salmon in a bowl, and add the sauce.
Place the lime slices on the top of the salmon.
Leave for 30 minutes.

Grease aluminum foil sections for each of the 4 salmon pieces.
Place the salmon pieces on aluminum foil; top each piece with lime slices and a shiitake mushroom, and pour 1 tablespoon sauce over. Close the tops of the aluminum foil, and grill for 10 minutes over a medium heat.
(You can also use a greased frying pan with a lid or an oven heated to 350° F.)

4-7: FRIED FISH IN HOT SAUCE

SERVES 4

1 pound tilapia fillet (or any ocean white fish, fresh or frozen)
¼ cup cornstarch
1 slightly beaten egg

Oil for deep-frying

SAUCE:
3 cloves garlic
½ hot pepper (or dash of red pepper)
1 tablespoon whisky
1 tablespoon white wine
1 tablespoon sugar
2½ tablespoons soy sauce
2 tablespoons vinegar

2 tablespoons vegetable oil

Cut the fillet into 1½-inch squares. (If you use frozen fish, cut into 1-inch cubes.)
Put the cubed fish in a bowl, and pour the egg and cornstarch over it. Coat well.

Heat the oil in a pan, and deep-fry the fish.
Drain the fish on a paper towel.

Chop the garlic and hot pepper.
Heat 2 tablespoons of oil in a pan, and sauté the garlic and hot pepper.
Pour the rest of the sauce ingredients into the pan. Bring to a boil.
Add the fried fish to the boiling sauce, carefully stirring so as not to break the pieces of fish. Cook for 1 minute.

4~8: RAW FISH (SASHIMI)

SERVES 4

This recipe is not one you can make with ingredients straight out of your refrigerator. Sashimi requires the right kind of fresh fish, because it is eaten raw.

If a fish is kosher, its sashimi (raw flesh) is also kosher. At various large supermarkets, raw salmon and raw tuna cuts are sold fresh enough to be eaten raw. However, for this particular food, I recommend visiting Japanese fish markets, where you will find a variety of fish and they will be fresh due to the high turnover. In addition, the fish will be completely prepared and cut to serve raw.

My recommendations of fish for sashimi are as follows:

SERVES 4

8 ounces tuna
      Red tuna (maguro)
      Fatty tuna (chu-toro)
      The most fatty tuna (oo-toro)
8 ounces salmon
6 ounces yellow tail
6 ounces yellow jack or fluke
Optional: ¼ white radish (daikon)

Cut fillet into thin rectangular slices ½ inch thick, 2 inches long, and 1 inch wide.
Arrange the sliced raw fish on a platter, and serve soy sauce with green mustard for dipping.
Optional: Shred the white radish (daikon).
Serve with plain rice, miso soup, and pickled cucumber.

A platter of raw fish also makes a nice appetizer.

4-9: FISH TERIYAKI

SERVES 4

1½ pounds of fresh tuna fillet (or swordfish or any other fish steak)

MARINADE:
1½ tablespoons soy sauce
1 tablespoon white wine
1 tablespoon sesame oil
(Or you can use ready-made kosher teriyaki sauce instead.)

Combine the ingredients for the marinade.

Marinate the fish fillet for 1 hour.

Grill the fish fillet, basting several times with the marinade. (The outside should be shiny brown.)

5. MEAT, POULTRY, AND EGGS

The preparation of meat dishes in Japan is different in several ways from the typical Western treatment. First, the basic seasoning is soy sauce instead of salt and pepper. Rice wine (sake), ginger, and garlic are mixed with the soy sauce. Most of the meat dishes are accompanied by plain white rice in Japan, and as a result, the seasoning may be a bit strong. If you are serving these dishes with seasoned rice or potatoes, you may wish to reduce the amount of soy sauce in each recipe.

Second, to make the meat convenient to eat with chopsticks, it is served in bite-size pieces. With a few exceptions, such as *teppan-yaki* steak, the meat is sliced thinly. If your butcher is cooperative, ask him to cut the meat into thin slices; if you have to slice the meat yourself, it will be easier to make thin slices if the meat is slightly frozen.

Third, portions served in Japan tend to be smaller than the amounts Americans are accustomed to eating.

Cutting meat into small pieces makes it easier to cook with vegetables, a favorite way of preparing meat in Japan. For example, in sukiyaki and *shabu-shabu* cooking, the meat is cooked in the same pot with a number of vegetables. In stir-fry cooking, the meat and vegetables are fried quickly over a high flame.

Locally produced beef in Japan is tender, tasty, and more expensive than imported frozen meat. Kobe beef is especially famous, and this type of meat is eaten thick.

Chicken is common in Japan, and is prepared much the same way as meat dishes: the same basic seasonings are used, and the chicken is cut into bite-size pieces.

Pork can be replaced by turkey; for instance, sweet and sour turkey.

5-1: SKEWERED BARBECUED CHICKEN (YAKI-TORI)

SERVES 4

1¼ pounds chicken breast or boneless thigh meat (depending on your
   preference)
2 leeks or 1 round onion
1 green pepper
8 white mushrooms
8 cherry tomatoes

SAUCE:
2 tablespoons sugar
3 tablespoons soy sauce
¾ teaspoon of salt
¼ cup white wine

Cut the chicken meat into 1½-inch cubes.
Cut the leeks into pieces 2 inches long. (If a round onion is used, cut into 8 sections
and then separate each into 2 pieces.)
Cut the green pepper into 8 sections.

Prepare 8 skewers. On each skewer, alternately place chicken pieces, pieces of leek (or
round onion), sections of green pepper, and mushrooms.

Grill all the skewers at the same time while basting them with the soy sauce mixture
at least 5 times. (If there is not enough sauce, make more using the same proportions.)
When the chicken and vegetable pieces are done, add cherry tomatoes and grill briefly
(only 1–2 minutes).

Serve with the rice of your choice.

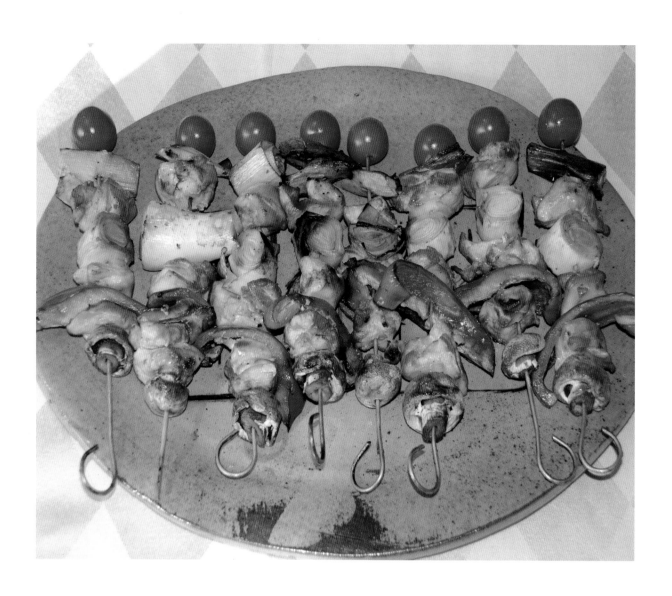

61

5-2: CHICKEN STEAMED IN WINE

SERVES 4

½ English cucumber
1 stalk of celery
4 strips of kosher wakame seaweed (optional)

1¼ pounds chicken thigh or breast meat
½ cup white wine or sherry

TEHINA SAUCE:
3 tablespoons Israeli-style tehina
1 teaspoon sugar
1 teaspoon white wine

LEMON SAUCE:
½ cup lemon juice
¼ cup soy sauce

Mustard

Julienne the cucumber and celery into 2-inch strips.
Soak the *wakame* in cold water for 15 minutes. Bring to a boil. Drain. Cool.

Put the chicken meat in a deep dish and cover with the wine or sherry.
Place the dish into a steamer, and steam for 15 minutes over a high flame. (*Do not put your hands in the steamer while cooking.*)
Cool the meat, and save the soup for other cooking.
Slice the chicken into ½-inch strips.
Serve cold with tehina sauce, lemon sauce, and mustard to dip the chicken.

5-3: CHICKEN TENDERS WITH MAYONNAISE SAUCE

SERVES 4

1 pound chicken tenders (or breast meat)
⅓ cup dry white wine
1 teaspoon powdered ginger (or 1 teaspoon grated fresh ginger)
2 stalks of green onion

MAYONNAISE SAUCE:
4 tablespoons mayonnaise
2 tablespoons white sesame seeds
1 tablespoon soy sauce
1 teaspoon vinegar

Put the chicken in a frying pan and cover with wine.
Bring to a boil and simmer for 10 minutes.
Pour the cooked chicken with the liquid into a shallow bowl, and cool. Tear the chicken into small pieces by hand.

Toast the sesame seeds and crush them. (see page 193) Mix with the other sauce ingredients and stir. Pour the sauce over the chicken pieces, mix well, and serve.

Cut the green onion into thin, small slices and use as garnish on top of the chicken pieces.

Serve cold.

5-4: FRIED CHICKEN WITH WALNUTS

1 pound chicken breast or thigh meat (depending on preference)
2 tablespoons cornstarch
1 slightly beaten egg
dash of powdered ginger

Oil for deep-frying

1½ tablespoons oil
1 round onion
1 green pepper
dash of salt
½ hot pepper (optional—if you like spicy food)
2 cloves of garlic, crushed

SAUCE
2 tablespoons soy sauce
1 tablespoon white wine★
1 teaspoon sugar★
★You may replace the wine and sugar with 1 tablespoon kosher mirin.

½ cup walnuts

Cube the chicken meat, and mix with the slightly beaten egg and cornstarch. Coat the chicken well with the batter.

Deep-fry the chicken meat until golden brown. Drain.

Cut the onion and green pepper into ½-inch squares.
Optional: Chop the hot pepper.

Heat 1½ tablespoons oil in a pan, and fry the green pepper, onion, and hot pepper with a dash of salt over a high flame, stirring continuously for a few minutes.
Combine all ingredients for the sauce, and add it together with the fried chicken and crushed garlic cloves. Stir well.

Add walnuts, and turn off the flame.

Note: Vegetables such as carrots or celery may be added or substituted instead of nuts.

5-5: JAPANESE CHICKEN NUGGETS

1 pound chicken breast
2 tablespoons soy sauce
⅓ teaspoon powdered ginger (or 1 teaspoon grated fresh ginger)
1 tablespoon dry wine★
1 teaspoon sugar★
★You may replace the wine and sugar with 1 tablespoon kosher mirin

1 egg
1 tablespoon white wine
½ cup flour

Oil for deep-frying

Cut the chicken into bite-size cubes.
Combine the soy sauce, wine, ginger, and sugar, and marinate the chicken in this mixture for 30 minutes.
Beat the egg slightly, and add the wine and extra marinade.
Combine the egg mixture with the flour.
Dip the chicken pieces in the batter.

Heat the oil in a pan, and fry the chicken pieces until brown. Drain.

Serve warm.

5-6: SWEET AND SOUR TURKEY

Serves 4

1 pound turkey meat (breast or thigh depending on preference)
2 tablespoons dry red wine
dash of powdered ginger
dash of salt

1 egg
5 tablespoons flour
1 teaspoon water

Oil for deep-frying

1 large round onion
1 carrot
⅓ head of cauliflower (or broccoli)
1 large green pepper
3 shiitake mushrooms (or 5 white mushrooms)
10 snow peas
4 slices of fresh or canned pineapple
3 tablespoons oil

Sauce:
¾ cup water
2 cloves garlic, crushed
3 tablespoons soy sauce
4 tablespoons vinegar
4 tablespoons sugar
3 tablespoons dry white wine
2 tablespoons cornstarch

Cut the turkey meat into 1-inch cubes, and marinate in the red wine with the ginger and salt for 30 minutes.

Dip the turkey meat in the mixture of egg, flour, and water. Deep-fry the turkey over a high flame until golden brown, then drain.

Cut the onion into 8 sections. Cut the carrots into thin slices. Break the cauliflower into small pieces. Slice the green pepper lengthwise. Slice the mushrooms. (Other vegetables can be substituted, for example, celery, cabbage, and leek.) Cut the pineapple slices into 4 sections.

Heat the oil in a frying pan (or a wok), and stir-fry over a high flame the onions, carrots, green peppers, and mushrooms, adding the cauliflower, snow peas, and turkey meat later. (The vegetables should not be fried more than a few minutes in order to retain their water and crispness.)
Place the vegetables and meat to the side.

Combine all the ingredients for the sauce in the frying pan, and bring to a boil. Add the meat and vegetables to the sauce; stir well, then remove from the flame. Pour into a serving dish. Garnish with the pineapple pieces on the top.

Note: Without the turkey, this makes a good vegetarian dish.

5-7: STEAMED WHOLE CHICKEN

SERVES 4

1 whole chicken
1 stalk of green onion
½ teaspoon powdered ginger, or 1 tablespoon grated fresh ginger
½ teaspoon salt
1 tablespoon soy sauce
½ cup vegetable oil

½ head of broccoli
6 ounces white mushrooms
1 carrot
3 leaves of Chinese cabbage or ordinary cabbage

SAUCE:
2 cloves garlic
2 tablespoons white wine or sherry
1 tablespoon soy sauce
1 stalk of green onion

Chop 2 stalks of green onion; leave half for the sauce.
Rub the whole chicken with salt, ginger, and chopped green onion. Let stand for 30 minutes.

Pour 1 tablespoon soy sauce over the chicken.
Heat ¼ cup oil in a large, deep pan, and fry the chicken until golden brown.

Slice the broccoli, mushrooms, carrot, and cabbage leaves in a bowl that fits in a steamer.

Crush the garlic and combine with the other sauce ingredients, and pour the sauce over the vegetables in the bowl.

Place the chicken atop the vegetables in the bowl, and steam for 1 hour. The chicken is done when clear juice runs out when pierced by a fork.

Serve the chicken with the vegetables. Add salt if necessary.

5-8: CHICKEN TERIYAKI

4 chicken thighs with skin and bones
4 chicken drumsticks
or
1½ pounds boneless, skinned chicken thigh meat

MARINADE:
4 garlic cloves, crushed
2 tablespoons soy sauce
2 tablespoons white wine or sherry
1 teaspoon sugar
1 tablespoon sesame oil

Combine the ingredients for the marinade.
Marinate the meat for 1 hour.
If you are using boneless, skinned meat, pour the sesame oil and mix just before placing on the grill.

Grill while basting with the remaining marinade.

5-9: TURKEY STEAK WITH GINGER

SERVES 4

1 pound turkey breast
3 purple cabbage leaves
1 tomato

MARINADE:
1 tablespoon grated fresh ginger, or ½ teaspoon powdered ginger
2 tablespoons soy sauce
1 tablespoon white wine or sherry★
1 tablespoon sugar★
1 tablespoon sesame oil
★You may substitute 1 tablespoon kosher mirin for the sherry and sugar.

Slice the turkey breast thinly (about ½-inch thick) into 4 pieces.
Shred the cabbage leaves with a knife, and place on 4 dinner plates.
Cut the tomato into sections, and place 3 sections on each of the 4 dinner plates.

Combine the ingredients for the marinade, and marinate the turkey pieces for 10 minutes.
Just before grilling, pour sesame oil on the turkey pieces.

Grill the turkey pieces, and serve with shredded cabbage and tomato pieces. You can also cut the meat into 1-inch strips and place them beside the cabbage.

5-10: JAPANESE SCHNITZEL (TONKATSU)

SERVES 4

2 cabbage leaves
1 tomato

1 pound turkey breast meat
1 tablespoon grated fresh ginger (or ½ teaspoon powdered ginger)
1 slightly beaten egg
breadcrumbs

Oil for deep-frying

SAUCE:
4 tablespoons Worcestershire sauce
1 tablespoon ketchup

or

3 tablespoons A1 sauce
3 tablespoons ketchup

or

4 tablespoons ketchup
3 tablespoons soy sauce
1 teaspoon sugar
1 teaspoon vinegar
dash of black pepper

Shred cabbage leaves with a knife, and place on 4 dinner plates.
Cut tomato into sections, and place 3 sections on each of the 4 dinner plates.

Slice the turkey breast meat thinly (about ½ inch thick) into 4 pieces.
Rub the meat with ginger.
Dip the turkey pieces one by one into the egg and then coat with breadcrumbs.
Deep-fry.
Drain the turkey; cut into 1-inch strips, and serve each piece next to the shredded cabbage and tomato sections.

Mix all ingredients for the sauce of your choice, and serve in a bowl to pour over the fried turkey and cabbage.

5-11: SCHNITZEL WITH CURRY SAUCE (KATSU CURRY)

¾ pound turkey breast meat
1 tablespoon grated fresh ginger (or ½ teaspoon powdered ginger)
1 slightly beaten egg
breadcrumbs

Oil for deep-frying

Curry sauce:
1 round onion
2 cloves garlic
½ hot pepper (optional—if you like it spicy)
2 carrots
5 ounces Brussels sprouts (fresh or frozen, 8 pieces)
2 tablespoons vegetable oil
3 teaspoons curry powder
3 tablespoons flour
2 teaspoons (or cubes) of chicken bouillon
3 cups water
¼ cup raisins

Slice the turkey breast meat thinly (about ½-inch thick) into 4 pieces.
Rub the meat with ginger.
Dip the turkey pieces into the egg and coat with breadcrumbs one by one.
Deep-fry.
Drain; place each piece on a plate, and cut the meat into 1-inch strips.

Chop the round onion and garlic (and hot pepper).
Slice the carrots.
Heat 2 tablespoons oil in a pan, and sauté the onion and garlic.
Add the carrots and Brussels sprouts.
Add the curry powder, bouillon, and flour, and mix well.
Pour water and bring to a boil, stirring constantly until the curry sauce becomes thick.
Reduce the heat and simmer for 10–15 minutes.

Place the turkey schnitzel strips on a dish with plain rice; pour the curry sauce over the meat.

5-12: ROASTED TURKEY (YAKI-BUTA)

SERVES 4

2 pounds turkey breast
2 tablespoons vegetable oil

MARINADE:
4 tablespoons white wine or sherry
⅓ cup soy sauce
3 tablespoons sugar
1 leek
2 tablespoons fresh grated ginger, or 1 teaspoon powdered ginger

Chop the leek, and combine all the ingredients for the marinade in a bowl, and marinate the turkey for 5 hours in the refrigerator.

Heat the oil in a deep pan, and fry the turkey until brown.
Pour the marinade into the pan, cover, and cook over a low heat for 50 minutes, periodically basting the meat with the marinade. (You may also use an oven at 350° F degrees.)

Cool the meat, then cut into thin slices. (You can also use the slices as a topping for noodle soups.)

5-13: BARBECUED BEEF WITH SESAME SEEDS

SERVES 4

2 pounds steak (boneless rib eye steak is best)

MARINADE
2 tablespoons white sesame seeds
3 cloves garlic, crushed
3 tablespoons soy sauce
3 tablespoons white or red wine★
1 teaspoon sugar★
★You may replace the wine and sugar with 3 tablespoons kosher mirin.

1 tablespoon sesame oil

Cut the beef into very thin slices.
Toast the sesame seeds, and crush. (see page 193) Mix all the ingredients for the marinade, and marinate the beef for at least 1 hour.

Just before grilling the meat, pour the sesame oil over the meat.
Grill the slices of beef 2 minutes to a side, more or less depending on preference.

Serve with your favorite rice and salad.

5-14: SPICY KOREAN-STYLE BARBECUE

SERVES 4

1½ pounds beef (steak)

MARINADE:
2 stalks of green onions
1 small hot pepper, or a few dashes of crushed red pepper
2 cloves garlic
4 tablespoons soy sauce
2 tablespoons sherry or white wine
2 tablespoons sugar
1 tablespoon sesame seeds
2 tablespoons oil

DIPPING SAUCE:
⅓ cup soy sauce
¼ cup sherry or white wine
2 tablespoons olive oil
2 stalks of green onion

Slice the beef very thinly by cutting while slightly frozen.
Chop the green onion and hot peppers.
Crush the garlic.
Toast the sesame seeds and crush. (see page 193)
Mix all the ingredients for the marinade, and marinate the beef for at least 1 hour.

Chop the green onion, and combine the ingredients for the sauce.
Grill the beef, and serve with the dipping sauce.

You can also grill vegetables, such as onion, leek, green peppers, and mushrooms, together with the meat and dip in the same sauce before eating.

5-15: BEEF ROLL

1½ pounds steak (boneless rib eye or beef shoulder for London broil)
2–3 tablespoons soy sauce

6–10 stalks of green onion, depending on size
2 tablespoons cornstarch

3 tablespoons flour
Oil for deep-frying

Optional; 1 grated white radish (daikon)
1 lemon
Soy sauce

Cut the beef into 12 thin slices about 4 inches square, and marinate in soy sauce for 30 minutes. It is easier to cut thinly when the beef is slightly frozen.

Cut the green onions into 4-inch-long pieces (the same length as the meat), dip in the cornstarch, and make 12 bunches, mixing green and white parts of the green onions.

Tightly wrap a slice of beef around each bunch of green onion.
Use toothpicks to keep the meat in place.

Coat the rolls with flour, and deep-fry for 3 minutes, then drain on absorbent paper.
Cut each roll into three pieces.

Optional: Peel and grate the daikon.
Cut the lemon into 8 pieces.
Serve the beef rolls hot with grated daikon, lemon, and soy sauce to taste.

Serve with your favorite rice.

5-16: BEEF WITH GREEN PEPPERS

1 pound beef (beef shoulder for London broil)
2 tablespoons white wine
2 tablespoons cornstarch

Oil for deep-frying

1½ green peppers
8 ounces bean sprouts
1 round onion

2 tablespoons vegetable oil

½ teaspoon salt
2 tablespoons soy sauce
1 tablespoon white wine
1 teaspoon cornstarch dissolved in 1 tablespoon water

Cut the beef very thin, and then cut into 2-inch-long strips.
Put the beef in a bowl, and marinate in white wine for 20 minutes.
Mix with the cornstarch, and deep-fry the beef for 1 minute at low heat. Drain.

Cut the green peppers and onion into thin 2-inch-long strips.
Wash the bean sprouts. Drain.
Heat 2 tablespoons vegetable oil in a frying pan, and quickly fry the green peppers and onion over a high flame. Add salt.
When the vegetables become soft, add the meat, and cook together for a few minutes.
Add the soy sauce and white wine.
Add the bean sprouts, and cook for 1 minute, and pour cornstarch dissolved in water.
When the cornstarch has thickened the sauce, remove from the flame.

5-17: GROUND BEEF WITH VEGETABLES

SERVES 4

1 pound ground beef
2 cloves garlic
1 green pepper
1 round onion
¼ head of cauliflower
1 carrot
⅓ cup white mushrooms
½ cup walnuts

2 tablespoons vegetable oil

½ teaspoon salt
2 tablespoons soy sauce
2 tablespoons dry white wine
1 teaspoon sugar
½ teaspoon vinegar

1 tablespoon cornstarch dissolved in 1 teaspoon water

3 iceberg lettuce leaves

Manually chop the garlic, green pepper, onion, cauliflower, carrot, mushrooms, and nuts. (*Do not use a food processor.*)

Pour the oil into a frying pan, and first sauté the garlic for 1 minute and then all the chopped vegetables, except the walnuts, for a few minutes over a high flame. Add salt, and sauté one more minute.
Add the ground beef, and sauté a few more minutes.
Add the rest of the seasoning to the meat and vegetables, and stir well over a high flame for 1 minute.
Add the cornstarch dissolved in water; stir well, and turn off the flame.
Add the chopped walnuts.

Place the food on top of the iceberg lettuce on a platter, and serve with your favorite rice.

5-18: TOFU AND GROUND BEEF

2 boxes of kosher tofu (12 ounces each)

1 pound ground beef
2 stalks of green onion
4 shiitake mushrooms
1½ tablespoons grated fresh ginger, or ½ teaspoon powdered ginger
2 cloves garlic, crushed
dash of red pepper
½ cup soup stock

2 tablespoons sesame oil

1 tablespoon kosher red miso
2 tablespoons soy sauce
1 teaspoon sugar

1 teaspoon cornstarch dissolved in 2 teaspoons water

Cut the tofu into 1-inch cubes.
Chop the green onions, and slice the mushrooms.

In a pan, pour 2 cups water, and bring to a boil.
Add the tofu cubes, and simmer for 3 minutes.
Leave the tofu in the hot water to keep warm.

Chop the green onion. Mix the red miso, soy sauce, and sugar in a small bowl.
Heat the oil in a frying pan, and fry the ground beef, green onion, and mushrooms with ginger powder, garlic, and red pepper for a few minutes.
Add the miso mixture to the frying pan, and stir well.
Add soup stock, and bring to a boil.
Remove the tofu from the hot water and add to the frying pan, and cook.
Add the cornstarch dissolved in water; stir until the sauce thickens, and remove from the flame.

5-19: BARBECUED BEEF WITH SOY SAUCE

SERVES 4

2 pounds steak (boneless rib eye steak is the best)
2 tablespoons soy sauce

1 white radish (daikon)
1 lemon
Soy sauce

Cut the beef into very thin slices. Marinate the meat in soy sauce for 10 minutes. Grill the beef slice by slice.

Peel the white radish and grate. Serve the white radish, sliced lemon, and soy sauce in the center of the table. Diners combine the ingredients according to preference to make their own sauce for the meat.

5-20: STUFFED MUSHROOMS

12–16 large fresh white mushrooms
½ pound ground beef
1 stalk of green onion
¼ teaspoon salt
1 tablespoon soy sauce
1 tablespoon white wine or sherry
½ teaspoon sugar
1 tablespoon cornstarch

2 tablespoons flour

Wash the mushrooms, and remove the stems.

Chop finely the stems and green onion, and mix with the meat and the rest of the ingredients.

Sprinkle flour inside the caps of the mushrooms, and fill the caps with the meat mixture.

Put all the stuffed mushrooms in a flat bowl. Steam for 15–20 minutes.

Serve hot or cold. Can be served as an appetizer.

5-21: STUFFED EGGPLANT

SERVES 4

2 Italian eggplants

½ pound ground beef
1 stalk of green onion
1 tablespoon grated fresh ginger (or ½ teaspoon powdered ginger)
1 tablespoon wine or sherry
¼ teaspoon salt
1 teaspoon soy sauce
1 teaspoon sesame oil
dash of black pepper

BATTER:
5 tablespoons flour
5 tablespoons cornstarch
3 tablespoons water
1 egg, slightly beaten
1 tablespoon soy sauce

Oil for deep-frying

Wash the eggplant, take off the stem, and slice lengthwise into ½-inch-thick slices.

Chop the green onion, and mix the ground beef with the rest of the ingredients.

Sandwich the beef between the eggplant slices.

Combine the ingredients for the batter.
Coat the sandwiched eggplants with the batter, and deep-fry. Drain.
Cut each eggplant in half and serve.

5-22: STUFFED GREEN PEPPERS

SERVES 4

1 pound ground beef
4 large green peppers
1 carrot
1 round onion

2 tablespoons olive oil

2½ tablespoons soy sauce
1 tablespoon white wine
1 egg
2 tablespoons olive oil

Carefully remove the seeds from the green peppers.
Chop the carrot and onion.
Sauté the meat and chopped vegetables, adding the sugar, soy sauce, and wine. Turn off the heat. Let cool.

Add the egg to the sautéed vegetables and meat, and mix well. Stuff each pepper with the mixture.

Put 2 tablespoons oil in a pan. Fry the green peppers over a low flame for 45 minutes. Keep the pan covered, but turn the peppers several times while cooking.

5-23: JAPANESE PLAIN OMELET

S*ERVES* 4

8 eggs
¼ cup chicken soup stock (see 2-1,a)
¼ teaspoon salt
½ teaspoon soy sauce
1 tablespoon white wine or sherry
½ teaspoon sugar

Nonstick cooking spray (vegetable oil)

Beat eggs, and add the rest of the ingredients.
Spray a frying pan with the cooking spray; heat the pan, then gently pour the egg mixture, spreading it over the pan.
Let rise. While the top is still soft, remove from the flame and then roll the egg in the pan.
Remove the rolled egg from the frying pan, and cut it into pieces.

5-24: EGG FU-YUNG

SERVES 4

6 eggs
4 stalks of green onion
6 shiitake mushrooms (or 8 white mushrooms)
3 ounces green peas
1 stalk of celery
1 tablespoon white wine or sherry
¼ teaspoon salt
½ teaspoon sugar
dash of black pepper

1 tablespoon vegetable oil

SAUCE:
1 cup chicken soup stock (see 2-1,a) or water
1 tablespoon soy sauce
1 teaspoon sugar
¼ teaspoon salt
1 teaspoon vinegar
2 tablespoons cornstarch

Mince the green onion, and shred the celery and mushrooms.
Combine the eggs, minced and shredded vegetables, and seasoning.
Divide the egg mixture into 4 portions.
Heat the oil in a frying pan.
Pour the divided egg mixture into the heated pan, shaping a round omelet 5 inches in diameter.
Cook 3 more omelets in the same way, adding oil each time.

Pour all the ingredients for the sauce into a small pan, and cook until thick.
Pour the sauce over the omelets.

Serve hot.

6. TABLE COOKING

In contrast to formal Japanese dinners, such as *kaiseki*, where a number of small dishes are served as individual courses to each person, table cooking offers an intimate atmosphere where all the food is cooked together in a large pot at the center of the table. The best-known cooking of this kind is sukiyaki. Such cooking is especially popular in Japan in winter. It is very cozy on a cold night to sit around the pot at the center of the table, cooking, talking, and eating the hot food. One could make a case that central heating, which is pervasive in today's Japan, is spoiling table cooking. I turn down the heat when I do table cooking, just as I do when I make a fire in our fireplace, to enjoy the ambience.

For table cooking, raw vegetables and meat or fish—carefully sliced and decoratively arranged—are served on large platters.

There are a couple of things to keep in mind when preparing the raw materials. The meat and vegetables should be sliced thinly so that they will cook quickly. Meat is easier to cut when slightly frozen. In addition, the size of the slices is determined by what can be handled comfortably by chopsticks.

The food can be cooked either on electric hot plates or portable gas burners. It is also possible to use an electric frying pan, but you need a reasonably high heat.

The diners are their own cooks. They put the ingredients into the pot, and, when cooked sufficiently, transfer the food to the small bowls placed in front of them. While the food is cooking, the diners can converse over drinks.

Table cooking is well suited to informal parties. By adjusting the amount of ingredients, a varying number of diners can be accommodated. Perhaps most important, once the hostess has prepared the meat and vegetables, she can sit at the table and enjoy the meal together with her guests.

6-1: SUKIYAKI

You'll need either a cast-iron skillet a few inches deep on a portable electric or gas stove, or an electric frying pan placed in the center of the dinner table. One option is to cook in a frying pan in the kitchen and serve the pan on a hot plate on the dining table.

SERVES 4

2 pounds boneless rib eye steak
2 leeks
4 stalks green onions
4 white mushrooms
4 shiitake mushrooms (or a quartered portobello mushroom)
⅓ head of cauliflower or broccoli
1 carrot
2 tablespoons vegetable oil

SUKIYAKI SAUCE:
½ cup soy sauce
⅓ cup sugar
½ cup water
½ cup white wine or sherry

4 eggs (optional)

Slice the beef as thinly as possible (or ask your butcher), and cut into bite-size pieces. (It is easier to slice the meat while it is slightly frozen.)
Slice the leeks and green onions on the bias into 2-inch-long pieces.
Trim the edges of the mushroom stems.
Cut the cauliflower or broccoli into bite-size pieces.
Slice the carrot into ¼-inch-thick bits.
Arrange the meat and vegetables attractively on a large platter, and place on the dinner table.
Place the cast-iron skillet on a portable gas or electric stove, or electric frying pan, in the center of the table. Heat the oil in the pan, and put some of the meat and vegetables in the pan. Pour a corresponding amount of sauce into the pan. Use a medium to high heat to prevent water issuing from the vegetables.

When the food is done, diners take meat and vegetables from the pan with chopsticks and put them in their own small bowls.

Traditionally, Japanese dip the food in a slightly beaten raw egg placed in an individual bowl.

Fill the skillet with more meat, vegetables, and soup that can cook while everyone is eating.

Serve with plain rice. It is fun to sit around the sukiyaki pot on a chilly winter's evening, cooking, talking, and, of course, eating.

6-2: SHABU-SHABU

SERVES 4

You'll need a deep pot, such as a fondue pot, on a portable electric or gas stove placed in the center of the dinner table.

1½ pounds boneless rib eye steak
8 Chinese cabbage (napa) leaves
2 leeks or one bunch of green onions (about 6 stalks)
4 white mushrooms
4 shiitake mushrooms (or quartered portobello mushroom)
⅓ head of cauliflower or broccoli (or any vegetable you prefer)

4–6 cups of water

DIPPING SAUCES:

SESAME SAUCE:
4 tablespoons white sesame seed
1 teaspoon mustard
1 teaspoon lemon juice
4 tablespoons soy sauce
1 tablespoon sugar
4 tablespoons white wine
4 tablespoons soup stock

SIMPLIFIED SESAME SAUCE:
4 tablespoons Israeli-style tehina
4 tablespoons soy sauce
1 teaspoon lemon juice

LEMON SAUCE:
½ cup soy sauce
½ cup lemon juice
½ cup freshly grated white radish (daikon) (optional)

Slice the beef as thinly as possible (or ask your butcher), and cut into bite-size pieces. (It is easier to slice the meat while it is slightly frozen.)

Cut the Chinese cabbage (napa) leaves into 2-inch-long pieces.
Slice the leeks or green onions slantwise into 2-inch-long pieces.
Trim the edges of the mushroom stems.
Cut the cauliflower or broccoli into bite-size pieces.
Arrange the meat and vegetables attractively on a large platter, and place on the dinner table.

Boil the water in the pan.

Make the dipping sauces.

Sesame sauce:
Toast the sesame seeds, and crush. (see page 193) Mix all the ingredients for the sesame sauce in a bowl, and divide into 4 small individual dishes.

Simplified sesame sauce:
Mix all the ingredients in a bowl, and divide into 4 small individual dishes.

Lemon sauce:
Mix all the ingredients for the lemon sauce in a bowl, and divide into 4 small individual dishes.

When the water in the pan is boiled, each person puts his or her beef and vegetables in the boiling water, cooks briefly, collects the food, and eats with one of the dipping sauces. The beef should not be cooked for more than a minute.

The name *shabu shabu* comes from the swishing sound made when the meat is placed in the water with chopsticks and moved from side to side.

While eating, fill the pot with more beef and vegetables. Serve with plain rice. This is a good winter dish for both family and company.

6-3: CHICKEN STEW (MIZUTAKI)

You'll need a deep pot, such as a fondue pot, on a portable electric or gas stove placed in the center of the dinner table.

SERVES 4

2 pounds chicken thigh meat with bones
8 Chinese cabbage (napa) leaves
2 stalks of leek, or one bunch (about 6 stalks) of green onions
4 white mushrooms
4 shiitake mushrooms (or quartered portobello mushroom)
⅓ head of cauliflower or broccoli
1 carrot
(Or any vegetable of your preference)

4–6 cups water

DIPPING SAUCES:

SESAME SAUCE:
4 tablespoons white sesame seeds
1 teaspoon mustard
1 teaspoon lemon juice
4 tablespoons soy sauce
1 tablespoon sugar
4 tablespoons white wine
4 tablespoons soup stock

SIMPLIFIED SESAME SAUCE:
4 tablespoons Israeli-style tehina
4 tablespoons soy sauce
1 teaspoon lemon juice

LEMON SAUCE:
½ cup soy sauce
½ cup lemon juice
½ cup freshly grated daikon (optional)

(Or any fondue dipping sauce of your preference)

Remove the skin from the thigh meat. Cut each thigh into 3 pieces. Put the meat in the pan filled with cold water. Without a cover, bring the water with the chicken pieces to a boil. Reduce the heat, and cook the chicken for 20 minutes over a medium flame. (If the flame is too strong, the chicken will become dry; if the flame is too weak, the meat will not separate from the bones easily.)
Cut the Chinese cabbage leaves into 3-inch-long slices.
Cut the leeks or green onions slantwise into 1-inch-long slices.
Trim the edges of the mushroom stems.
Cut the cauliflower or broccoli into bite-size pieces.
Slice the carrots.
Arrange the meat and vegetables attractively on a large platter, and place on the dinner table.

Make the dipping sauces.

Sesame sauce:
Toast the sesame seeds, and crush. (see page 193) Mix all the ingredients for the sesame sauce in a bowl, and divide into 4 small individual dishes.

Simplified sesame sauce:
Mix all the ingredients in a bowl, and divide into 4 small individual dishes.

Lemon sauce:
Mix all the ingredients for the lemon sauce in a bowl, and divide into 4 small individual dishes.

Diners should have their own individual dishes for the dipping sauce.

After cooking the chicken pieces in the boiling water, increase the heat slightly and add some vegetables. Each diner picks up chicken pieces and vegetables and dips in the sauces.

While eating, fill the pot with more vegetables. Serve with plain rice. This is a good winter dish for both family and company.

6-4: FISH STEW

You'll need a deep pot, such as a fondue pot, on a portable electric or gas stove placed in the center of the dinner table.

SERVES 4

1½ pounds cod fillet (or any other white meat fish fillet, e.g., haddock)
12 ounces kosher tofu (or egg tofu; see 1-2)
1 section (3 inches long) of Chinese cabbage (napa)
1 leek
2 green onions
1 radish
1 carrot

5½ cups kombu soup stock (see 2-1,b) or water
½ cup white wine or sherry

DIPPING SAUCE:
⅓ cup soy sauce
½ cup lemon juice
½ cup freshly grated white radish (daikon) (optional)

Cut the fish fillet into 2-inch squares.
Cut the tofu into 1-inch cubes.
Cut the Chinese cabbage leaves, leek, and green onion into pieces 2 inches long.
Slice the radish and carrot.
Arrange the fish and vegetables on a platter, and place on the table.

Place a pot with the soup stock (or water) on a stove in the center of the table.
Bring the soup stock (or water) to a boil.
Put the cabbage in the center of the pot and arrange the fish and other vegetables around the cabbage.

Combine all the ingredients for the dipping sauce, and divide into four individual bowls. As the fish and vegetables cook, eat them with the dipping sauce.

While eating, fill the pot with more vegetables. Serve with plain rice. This is a good winter dish for family and company.

6-5: TROUT STEW

You'll need a skillet (made of iron and a few inches deep) or a frying pan on a portable electric or gas stove placed in the center of the dinner table. Alternatively, you may also use an electric frying pan.

SERVES 4

1½ pounds trout fillet with skin
¼ teaspoon salt

3 potatoes
1 carrot
1 round onion
1 leek
6 Chinese cabbage (napa) leaves
2 tablespoons vegetable oil

SAUCE:
⅓ cup soy sauce
½ cup white wine
4 cups kombu soup stock (see 2-1,b)

Cut the trout into 2-inch pieces. Sprinkle with salt.

Pare the potatoes; slice them thinly, parboil, and drain.
Slice the carrot.
Cut the onions into 8 sections.
Cut the leek into 2-inch long pieces.
Cut the cabbage into 2-inch pieces.
Arrange the fish and the vegetables decoratively on a platter, and set on the table.

Place a pot on the stove or the electric frying pan in the center of the table.
Heat the oil in the pot; fry the onion and cabbage first.
Pour the sauce mixture into the pot, and add some of the fish and vegetables.
When the food is done, diners help themselves, taking fish, vegetables, and sauce to their individual plates. As everyone is eating, fill the pot with more trout and vegetables.

6-6: STEAK FRIED ON IRON (TEPPAN-YAKI)

You'll need a large, flat skillet on a portable electric or gas stove, or an electric frying pan, placed in the center of the dinner table. One option is to cook in a frying pan in the kitchen and serve the pan on a hot plate on the dining table.

SERVES 4

2 pounds rib eye steak
2 round onions
2 green peppers
8 white mushrooms
3 tablespoons vegetable oil

RADISH SAUCE:
1 white radish (daikon)
3 stalks green onions
½ cup soy sauce
½ cup lemon juice

SESAME SAUCE:
1 stalk green onion
1 clove garlic
2 tablespoons sesame
5 tablespoons soy sauce
1 tablespoon sugar
3 tablespoons white wine
1 tablespoon Israeli-style tehina

Cut the beef into 1-inch cubes.
Cut the onion into rings ½-inch thick.
Cut the green peppers into sections.
Trim the edges of the mushroom stems.
Arrange the meat and vegetables attractively on a platter, and place on the table.

Make the radish sauce as follows:
Peel and grate the white radish *(daikon)* and chop the green onion, and place on the table. Serve the soy sauce and lemon juice separately.

Make the sesame sauce as follows:
Chop the green onion and garlic. Toast the sesame seeds, and crush while hot. (see page 193) Combine them with the rest of the ingredients in a bowl, and place on the table.

Place a flat pan on the portable stove placed in the center of the table (or use an electric frying pan).
Heat the oil, and fry the meat and vegetables. Diners fry their own food and dip it in either radish sauce or sesame sauce in a small dish in front of them.

The meat and vegetables can be cooked in the kitchen and brought to the table hot.

6-7: KOREAN BARBECUE (KARUBI)

You'll need a portable grill placed in the center of the dinner table.

SERVES 4

2 pounds beef steak (rib eye steak is the best)
1 green pepper
1 round onion
1 leek
1 Italian eggplant (4 ounces)
1 carrot
1 portobello mushroom

MARINADE:
1 teaspoon white wine or sherry
½ teaspoon sugar
1 teaspoon sesame oil
1 tablespoon soy sauce
1 tablespoon sesame seeds, toasted and crushed
2 cloves garlic, crushed
Black pepper

DIPPING SAUCE:
½ cup soy sauce
2 tablespoons red wine
6 tablespoons water
1 tablespoon sugar
1 clove garlic, crushed
½ lemon, squeezed

Slice the beef thinly into 2–3-inch pieces.

Combine all the ingredients for the marinade, and marinate for about 20 minutes.

Combine all the ingredients for the dipping sauce, and divide into 4 individual dishes.

Cut the green pepper into 8 sections. Slice the onion in rings. Cut the leek into pieces 1½ inches long, and slice the eggplant, carrot, and mushroom thinly.

Place the meat and vegetables on platters.

Each diner will grill meat and vegetables on the tabletop grill and eat with dipping sauce when it is finished.

Serve with your favorite rice.

6-8: TOFU STEW (YUDOUFU)

This is a traditional vegetarian dish popular among Buddhist monks in Japan.

You'll need a deep pot, such as a fondue pot, on a portable electric or gas stove placed in the center of the dinner table. You'll also need a slotted spoon to pick up the pieces of tofu from the water.

SERVES 4

2 packages of kosher tofu (about 13 ounces each)
8 Chinese cabbage (napa) leaves
2 leeks, or one bunch (about 6 stalks) green onions
4 white mushrooms
4 shiitake mushrooms (or quartered portobello mushroom)
⅓ head of cauliflower or broccoli
1 carrot
(Add or substitute any vegetable of your preference)

4–6 cups kombu soup stock (see 2-1,b) or water

DIPPING SAUCES:

MISO SAUCE:
4 tablespoons red miso
1 tablespoon sugar (or honey)
1 tablespoon white sesame seeds
1 tablespoon white wine

TEMPURA SAUCE:
⅓ cup wine (red or white)
⅓ cup soy sauce
⅓ cup sugar
⅓ cup water

118

LEMON SAUCE:

½ *cup soy sauce*

½ *cup lemon juice*

Optional: ½ *cup freshly grated white radish (daikon)*

Cut the tofu into pieces about 1½ inches square.

Slice the Chinese cabbage leaves into 2-inch-long pieces.
Slice the leeks or green onions on the bias into 2-inch lengths.
Trim the mushroom stems.
Cut the cauliflower or broccoli into bite-size pieces.
Cut the carrots into thin 2-inch-long pieces.
Arrange the tofu and vegetables attractively on a large platter, and place on the dinner table.

Make the dipping sauces.

Miso sauce:
Toast the sesame seeds, and crush. (see page 193) Mix all the ingredients for the miso sauce in a bowl, and divide into 4 small individual dishes.

Tempura sauce:
Mix all the ingredients in a bowl, boil the sauce, and cool it. Divide the sauce into 4 small individual dishes.

Lemon sauce:
Mix all the ingredients for the lemon sauce in a bowl, and divide into 4 small individual dishes.

When the water in the pot is boiled, each diner puts his or her tofu and vegetables in the boiling water, cooks briefly, removes, and dips in one of the sauces. While eating, fill the pot with more tofu and vegetables. This is a good winter dish for both family and company.

6-9: MIXED STEW (YOSE-NABE)

You'll need a deep pot, such as a fondue pot, on a portable electric or gas stove placed in the center of the dinner table.

Serves 4

½ pound boneless chicken breast
½ pound boneless chicken thigh
15 ounces tofu
4 sprigs Italian parsley
4 bunches of fresh spinach (or 5 ounces frozen leaf-spinach)
4 Chinese cabbage leaves
1 leek
4 shiitake mushrooms
1 carrot
4 ounces bamboo shoots (optional)

4 cups water
1 teaspoon salt
1 tablespoon soy sauce
2 tablespoons sherry or white wine
1 teaspoon sugar

DIPPING SAUCE A:
4 tablespoons soy sauce
4 tablespoons lemon juice

DIPPING SAUCE B:
4 tablespoons soy sauce
4 tablespoons Israeli-style tehina
1 teaspoon sugar

Cut the chicken meat into 2-inch pieces.

Dice the tofu into 2-inch pieces.

Cut the parsley, spinach, and cabbage leaves into pieces 2 inches in length.

Cut the leek into 2-inch slanted pieces.

Slice the mushrooms, carrot, and bamboo shoots.

In a large pot placed in the center of the table, pour the water with salt, soy sauce, wine, and sugar, and bring to a boil.

Place the chicken pieces first into the pot, and cook for 15 minutes over a medium heat.

Add the vegetables.

Mix all ingredients for dipping sauces, and serve individually.

As the meat and vegetables finish, each diner selects food and eats with the dipping sauces.

Yosenabe means a pot with assorted ingredients, and you may use any ingredients you prefer.

7. VEGETABLES

When I lived in Israel, I took pleasure in the variety of fresh vegetables available, as in Japan. In Jerusalem, where my husband and I lived for seven years, there was a wonderful outdoor market called Mahane Yehuda. We used to get large baskets to shop for crispy vegetables.

Frying vegetables in a pan over a high flame not only makes the food taste good but also preserves the nutrients in the vegetables. The technique of frying quickly at a high heat also prevents the vegetables from becoming watery, which tends to occur when vegetables are cooked at low temperatures. In general, we eat much vegetable cooking in Japan. Cooked vegetables served warm make nice vegetarian dishes.

7-1: TEMPURA

Serves 4

TEMPURA DIPPING SAUCE:
⅓ cup soy sauce
⅓ cup sugar
⅓ cup red wine
⅓ cup water
Freshly grated white radish (daikon) (optional)

TEMPURA INGREDIENTS:
4 white mushrooms
4 shiitake mushrooms (or any mushroom, e.g., portobello mushroom)
1 baby eggplant (to make 8 slices)
1 small green pepper
16 string beans
⅓ small yam (to make 8 thin slices)
⅛ head of broccoli
4 pieces of seaweed (nori) cut into 2 × 3-inch sections (optional)
½ pound of lemon sole or flounder fillet or any white fish fillet
   (optional)

Oil for deep-frying

BATTER:
1 egg
1 cup cold water
1 cup sifted flour

TEMPURA DIPPING SAUCE:
Boil all the ingredients for the tempura dipping sauce except the white radish *(daikon)*, and cool. Pour into 4 small individual bowls. *Optional:* Add grated white radish *(daikon)* when you eat.

Tempura ingredients:
Wash the vegetables, and drain well. Trim the edges of the mushroom stems. Cut the eggplant into ¼-inch slices. Cut the green pepper into 8 sections. Trim the edges of the string beans. Peel the yam and cut it into ¼-inch slices. Break the broccoli into bite-size pieces.

Cut the fish fillet into 3 × 2-inch sections.
Heat the oil for deep-frying in a large pot to 355° F.

Batter:
Mix the egg, cold water, and sifted flour in a bowl, and manually beat the mixture. The batter should be made just before frying.

Dip the tempura ingredients into the batter and immediately cook in the oil until golden brown. Drain on a paper towel.

Serve hot.

Note: Freshly made batter and the right oil temperature ensure light and crispy tempura.

Traditional Japanese cuisine is water-based. However, there are a few exceptions, such as tempura and sukiyaki, which reflect the Western influence on Japan after the country was opened in the late nineteenth century. Hanukkah is a celebration of oil, and tempura is a good fit for the chilly holiday season. Although it is deep-fried, tempura is not greasy as long as you use freshly made batter and the proper oil temperature (355° F).

7-2: CHINESE STYLE VEGETABLES (CHOP SUEY)

SERVES 4

1 round onion
½ green pepper
1 carrot (or 1 bamboo shoot)
4 Chinese cabbage (napa) leaves
4 shiitake mushrooms, or 4 white mushrooms
1 squash
¼ head of cauliflower (5 ounces)
¼ head of broccoli (4 ounces)
15 snow peas

2 tablespoons oil

SAUCE:
1 cup soup stock or water
1 tablespoon soy sauce
2 tablespoons white wine
1 teaspoon salt
1 teaspoon sugar
1 teaspoon vinegar
2 garlic cloves, crushed
2 tablespoons cornstarch dissolved in 2 tablespoons water

Peel the onion; cut into 8 sections.
Cut the green pepper into bite-size pieces.
Peel the carrot and slice it.
Slice the cabbage (*napa*) leaves, mushrooms, and squash.
Break the cauliflower and broccoli into bite-size pieces.

Heat the oil in a large frying pan.
Fry over a high flame the onion, green pepper, and carrot first, and then the cabbage (*napa*), mushrooms, squash, cauliflower, broccoli, and snow peas, stirring continuously.

Pour all the ingredients for the sauce, except the cornstarch, over the vegetables, and bring to a boil.
Add the cornstarch to the vegetables. Cook over a high flame for a few minutes, stirring continuously. When the sauce thickens, stop the heat. *Be careful not to overcook.*

This is a good vegetarian dish. However, you can also enrich the taste by frying 6 ounces of dark chicken meat for a few minutes over a high flame before adding the vegetables.

7-3: CUCUMBER AND EGGPLANT IN CHILI SAUCE

SERVES 4

3 cucumbers
1 pound eggplant (1 large eggplant or 3 Italian eggplants)
1 hot pepper, or dash of crushed hot pepper
2 cloves garlic

3 tablespoons vegetable oil

⅓ teaspoon salt

SAUCE:
2 tablespoons soy sauce
2 tablespoons water
1½ tablespoons sugar
2 tablespoons dry white wine
2 tablespoons cornstarch dissolved in 3 tablespoons water
1 tablespoon vinegar

Peel the cucumbers. Dice the cucumbers and eggplant. Chop the hot pepper and garlic.

Combine the ingredients for the sauce.

Heat the oil in a frying pan (or wok), and sauté the garlic and hot pepper over a medium flame. Add the cucumbers and eggplant, and sprinkle salt over the ingredients.

When the eggplant becomes soft, add the sauce; mix well, and extinguish the flame.

Serve hot or cold.

7-4: EGGPLANT COOKED IN SESAME OIL

SERVES 4

1 pound eggplant (3 Italian eggplants or 1 big eggplant)
3 tablespoons sesame oil
1 tablespoon soy sauce

Wash eggplant(s), and cut into slices about ¼ inch thick and 5 inches long.

Heat frying pan with 1 tablespoon sesame oil.
Place the eggplant slices evenly in the frying pan, and reduce the heat.
Pour 2 tablespoons sesame oil and 1 tablespoon soy sauce over the eggplant slices.
Cover the frying pan, and cook over a slow fire for 15–20 minutes—until the eggplant slices are well cooked.

Serve hot or cold.

7-5: BROILED MUSHROOMS

SERVES 4

16 white mushrooms

MARINADE:
1 teaspoon sugar
1 tablespoon soy sauce
2 tablespoons white wine or sherry

½ lemon

Wash the mushrooms, take off the stems, and marinate for 30 minutes.
Broil the mushrooms for 3–5 minutes, basting several times with the extra marinade.
Squeeze lemon juice over the mushrooms before serving.

7-6: CHILLED SWEET AND SOUR CUCUMBER

SERVES 4

3 cucumbers (1½ pounds)
½ teaspoon salt
1 teaspoon sugar

6 white mushrooms
½ green pepper
dash of red pepper
1 teaspoon sesame
⅓ teaspoon powdered ginger
1 tablespoon vegetable oil

1 tablespoon sugar
1 tablespoon white wine
1 tablespoon vinegar
1 teaspoon soy sauce
1 tablespoon cornstarch dissolved in 2 tablespoons water

Peel the cucumbers, and cut into sections 2 inches long and then lengthwise into quarters.
Sprinkle salt over the cucumber. Let stand for 30 minutes.
Rinse off the salt with water. Pour ½ teaspoon salt and 1 teaspoon sugar over the cucumbers.

Slice the mushrooms.
Cut the green pepper into 8 sections.

Heat the oil in a pan, and sauté the green peppers and mushrooms with the red pepper and sesame for 2 minutes. Add the remaining seasoning and cornstarch. When the sauce becomes thick, remove from heat.

Combine with the cucumber, and chill for 30 minutes in the refrigerator before serving.

7-7: SEA VEGETABLE (HIZIKI) AND MUSHROOMS

SERVES 4

1 cup dried hiziki (a sea vegetable hand-harvested wild)
8–10 shiitake mushrooms (dried shiitake soaked in water is better)

2 tablespoons sesame oil

3 tablespoons sugar
2 tablespoons soy sauce
1 teaspoon white wine
½ cup soup stock

Wash the *hiziki*, and soak for 10 minutes in 4 cups of cold water. Drain.
Slice the mushrooms into narrow strips.

In a frying pan, heat the oil, and fry the *hiziki* over a high flame for a few minutes.
Add the mushrooms, then fry another 1 minute, and turn off the flame.

Add the soup stock with sugar, soy sauce, and wine into the frying pan. Bring to a boil, and then cook over a low flame for 15 minutes. Remove the lid early on so that excess water will evaporate.

Serve at room temperature.

Hiziki is a health food. You can buy kosher *hiziki* at a health food store or order it from Eden in California.

8. RICE

Traditional Japanese rice is white and sticky, different from rice in China and elsewhere in Asia. It is eaten plain, especially on formal occasions, and its blandness is meant to contrast with the other dishes. As plain as it is, the Japanese in general are fussy about the quality of their rice. There are, however, a number of ways to cook rice for more casual occasions, as the recipes indicate. Whatever the seasonings that may be added to rice, it is never eaten in a sweetened form. Western-style dessert rice pudding is not part of the Japanese diet.

Mixed rice is an easy-to-make and tasty dish for casual occasions. *Donburi*, named after the large pottery bowl in which it is served, is a popular Japanese rice dish consisting of hot rice topped with egg, meat, and vegetables. The *donburi* bowl, which is deeper than a Western soup bowl, is also used for noodles, but any large Western soup bowl or cereal bowl can easily replace it.

Another favorite rice dish in Japan is sushi, which may be shaped into balls or topped with raw fish mixed with vegetables or rolled in seaweed called *nori-maki*. Although sushi with raw fish is becoming a luxury in Japan, there are other kinds of sushi that make good picnic lunches. Kosher seaweed is available at many markets in the United States.

While the Japanese tend to like white Japanese rice (e.g., Nishiki), you can use any rice of your preference, including brown rice, as the starch accompaniment to the dishes in this cookbook.

8-1: BASIC RICE

a. PLAIN RICE:

SERVES 4

2 cups uncooked kosher white Japanese rice (e.g., Nishiki rice)
2¾ cups water

Rinse the rice several times until the water becomes clear. Drain.
Add 2¾ cups water. Let stand for 30 minutes (to allow rice to absorb the water).

Bring the rice to a boil and gradually reduce the heat. The entire cooking process takes 20–30 minutes. *Do not remove the lid from the pot while cooking.*

After extinguishing the flame, leave the rice in the pot with the lid on for another 15 minutes.
With a spatula, stir the rice gently so that the rice will be soft and fluffy.

b. SUSHI RICE:

SERVES 4

2 cups uncooked Japanese kosher plain rice (e.g., Nishiki rice)
2 cups water

¼ cup vinegar
1½ tablespoons sugar
¾ teaspoon salt

Prepare the rice in the same manner as in the recipe for plain rice.
Combine the vinegar, sugar, and salt, and pour over the rice while it is still hot. Mix well.

8-2: SUSHI ROLLS (MAKI)

You'll need a sushi roller—a sheet 9 inches square made of bamboo. (see page 193)

SERVES 4

5 cups cooked sushi rice (see 8-1,b)
4 pieces kosher seaweed (approximately 7 × 8 inches)

SALMON FILLING:
5 ounces smoked salmon
1 ripe avocado

SEAFOOD FILLING:
5 ounces imitation crabmeat
¼ English cucumber (about 3 ounces)

Place the salmon filling.

Roll by lifting the sushi roller.

Roll from your side.

Press the rice firmly.

Cut all filling ingredients into long, narrow strips to fill the 8-inch width of the seaweed.

Open the sushi roller on the counter.
Place a wet paper towel on top of the sushi roller (so that the seaweed will not stick to the roller).
Place a sheet of seaweed on top of the paper towel.
Spread a cup of rice on the seaweed, leaving a 1-inch border on both sides of the seaweed.
Place the salmon and avocado filling on the rice.
Roll by lifting the sushi roller from your side towards the other, pressing the rice as you roll.
Open the roller, and push in the two ends.
Place the rolled sushi on a cutting board. Thinly cut off the two ends to be even.
Wet the knife with water and cut the rolled sushi into 1-inch-thick pieces. Keep on wetting the knife as you cut to prevent the rice from sticking to the knife.

Repeat for the remaining 3 rolls using both the salmon and seafood.
Serve with soy sauce and wasabi.

You can use any filling of your choice.

8-3: GREEN PEA RICE

SERVES 4

1 cup uncooked white Japanese rice (e.g., Nishiki rice)
1 cup frozen peas
1¼ cups water

Dash of table salt, or according to preference

Rinse the rice several times until the water becomes clear.
Drain. Add 1¼ cups of water. Let stand for 30 minutes (to allow rice to absorb the water).
Add the peas.

Bring the rice to a boil and gradually reduce the heat. The entire cooking process takes 20–30 minutes. *Do not remove the lid from the pot while cooking.*

After extinguishing the flame, leave the rice in the pot with the lid on for another 15 minutes.
With a spatula, stir the rice gently so that it will be soft and fluffy.

8-4: HAND-ROLLED SUSHI (NIGIRI)

This recipe requires sashimi (see 4-9)

SERVES 4

4-6 cups cooked sushi rice (see 8-1,b)

12 pieces raw tuna fish cut into rectangles of 1 × 3 × ½-inch (see 4-9)

8 pieces of raw salmon cut into rectangles of 1 × 3 × ½-inch (see 4-9)
8 pieces of yellow tail cut into rectangles of 1 × 3 × ½-inch (see 4-9)
8 pieces of fluke or yellow jack cut into rectangles of 1 × 3 × ½-inch
  (see 4-9)
8 pieces of 1 × 3 × ½-inch omelet (see 5-23)

Make oval rice balls as follows:
Dip both hands into water (so that the rice won't stick to your hands), and take a small handful of rice, holding it gently in your left hand.
Work the rice with your right hand, gently forming an oval shape with a flat top and bottom.
Top with the raw fish and omelet.
Serve with soy sauce and wasabi.

Restaurants often serve *nigiri* with the appetizer sushi rolls (see 1-11)

8-5: MIXED SUSHI (CHIRASHI)

SERVES 4

4–6 cups cooked sushi rice (see 8-1,b)

1 carrot
4 shiitake mushrooms (or 1 portobello mushroom, quartered)
½ cup water
3 tablespoons sugar
2 tablespoons soy sauce

4 pieces of 1 × 3 × ½-inch omelet (see 5-23)
2 sheets of seaweed

4 pieces raw tuna fish cut into rectangles of 1 × 3 × ½-inch (see 4-9)
8 pieces of raw salmon cut into the samesized rectangles as tuna (see 4-9)

OPTIONAL:
4 pieces of yellow tail cut into the same-sized rectangles as tuna (see 4-9)
4 pieces of yellow jack or fluke cut into the same-sized rectangles as tuna (see 4-9)

Cut the carrot into 2-inch-long pieces, and then cut lengthwise and again into narrow strips.

Slice the mushrooms.

In a pan, boil the water, sugar, and soy sauce, and cook the carrot pieces and mushroom slices without a lid for 10 minutes. Drain.

Cut the seaweed sheets with a shears into 2-inch strips of the same length as the carrots.

Divide the sushi rice into 4 large individual bowls.

Arrange the ingredients decoratively on top of the rice in each bowl.

If you use raw fish, serve with a small dish of soy sauce with wasabi so that each diner can dip the raw fish in the sauce.

Chirashi means "scattered toppings".

8-6: MIXED RICE

SERVES 4

4 ounces boneless chicken meat
6 shiitake mushrooms (or any other mushrooms)
1 8-ounce can of water chestnuts
1 carrot

2 cups uncooked white Japanese rice (e.g., Nishiki rice)
2½ cups water

2 tablespoons soy sauce
1 tablespoon white wine
1 teaspoon sugar

Cut the chicken meat into small pieces.
Thinly slice the mushrooms and water chestnuts.
Cut the carrots into 2-inch-long pieces, then thinly slice lengthwise, and then cut into narrow 2-inch pieces.

Rinse the rice several times until the water becomes clear.
Drain. Add 2½ cups water. Let stand for 30 minutes (to allow rice to absorb the water).

Add the chicken, vegetables, soy sauce, wine, and sugar to the rice.
Bring the rice to a boil and gradually reduce the heat. The entire cooking process takes 20–30 minutes. *Do not remove the lid from the pot while cooking.*

After turning off the flame, leave the rice in the pot with the lid on for another 15 minutes.
With a spatula, stir the rice gently so that it will be soft and fluffy.

If you have a rice cooker, prepare the rice in the same way as plain white rice and simply add the ingredients.

8-7: FRIED RICE

---

4 ounces chicken meat or kosher hot dogs
1 round onion
3 stalks of green onion
1 carrot
½ cup frozen green peas
2 tablespoons vegetable oil

3 slightly beaten eggs
Nonstick vegetable oil spray

2 cups white cooked rice (see 8-1,a)

1 teaspoon salt
1 tablespoon soy sauce
dash of powdered ginger
dash of powdered garlic
dash of black pepper

Fresh parsley

Cut the meat, onion, and green onion into small pieces.
Slice the carrot thinly.

Spray frying pan with non-stick spray, and fry the eggs; put to the side.

Heat 2 tablespoons oil in the frying pan. Fry the meat first, then the onion, green onion, and carrot.
Add the rice and peas, and cook.
Add the seasoning and finally the eggs. Stir well, and extinguish the flame.

Garnish with parsley.

8~8: CHICKEN AND EGG –TOPPED RICE (OYAKO-DONBURI)

SERVES 4

4–6 cups cooked white rice (see 8-1,a)

8 ounces chicken meat
2 stalks of green onions
4 stalks of Italian parsley
1 carrot
4 shiitake mushrooms
1 round onion

2 tablespoons vegetable oil

4 eggs
1 cup chicken soup stock or water
¼ cup soy sauce
¼ cup white wine
¼ cup sugar

Cut the chicken meat into small pieces.
Cut the green onions and Italian parsley into pieces 2 inches long.
Slice the carrot and mushrooms thinly.
Cut the onion vertically into narrow pieces.

Slightly beat the eggs, and combine with the soup stock, soy sauce, wine, and sugar.

Heat the oil in a frying pan, and fry the chicken first and then the vegetables.
When done, pour the egg mixture, reduce the heat, cover the frying pan, and cook until eggs are firm.

Divide the rice into 4 large bowls.
Place the egg mixture on top of the rice in each bowl.

Serve hot.

8-9: TEMPURA ON RICE (TEN-DON)

SERVES 4

6 cups cooked white rice (see 8-1,a)

TEMPURA:
4 shiitake mushrooms (or any mushrooms)
8 slices of eggplant
½ green pepper
12 string beans
4 pieces of seaweed (nori) cut into 2 × 3-inch rectangles (optional)
6 ounces of lemon sole or flounder fillet or any white fish fillet
*   (optional)*

BATTER:
1 egg
1 cup cold water
1 cup sifted flour

Oil for deep-frying

SAUCE:
⅓ cup chicken soup stock or water
⅓ cup soy sauce
⅓ cup white or red wine
¼ cup sugar

Trim the edges of the mushroom stems.
Cut the green pepper into 4 sections.
Trim the edges of the string beans.

Mix the egg and cold water, and blend the flour lightly.
Add the vegetables and fish to the batter, and mix.
Heat the oil for deep-frying in a deep pot to 355° F, and deep-fry until brown and crispy. Drain on a paper towel.

Put all the ingredients for the sauce in a pot, and bring to a boil. Cool.

Place the hot rice in 4 large individual bowls; place the tempura pieces on top of the rice, and pour the sauce over the tempura according to taste.

8–10: OMELET RICE

---

4 ounces boneless chicken meat
1 round onion
4 shiitake mushrooms (or any other mushroom)
1 carrot
½ cup frozen green peas

2 tablespoons vegetable oil

3 cups cooked white rice (see 8-1,a)

dash of salt
dash of black pepper
1 tablespoon barbecue sauce

8 eggs
Nonstick vegetable oil spray

4 tablespoons ketchup
4 parsley leaves

Cut the chicken meat into small pieces.
Chop the onion.
Slice the mushrooms and carrot.

Heat the oil in a frying pan, and fry the chicken meat first and then the onion, mush-
rooms, carrot, and green peas.
When everything is done, add the rice, and continue cooking.
Add dash of black pepper and of salt.
Add the barbecue sauce; stir some more, and extinguish the flame.

Slightly beat 2 eggs in a bowl.

Spray a small frying pan with nonstick vegetable oil, and heat.

Pour the eggs and make a thin omelet 9 inches in diameter.

On one side of the omelet, place ¼ portion of the mixed rice; fold over the other side of the omelet, and extinguish the flame.

Repeat this process for the rest of the 3 rice-omelets.

Garnish each rice-omelet dish with ketchup and parsley.

8-11: LUNCH BOX (BENTO)

---

2 cups cooked white Japanese rice
2 kosher umeboshi
1 piece of kosher seaweed (nori)

¼ pound chicken breast meat or boneless thigh meat (depending on
    your preference)
½ stalk of leek (or ¼ round onion)
½ green pepper

MARINADE:
1 tablespoon soy sauce
1 teaspoon sugar★
1 tablespoon white wine★
★You may replace the sugar and white wine with 1 tablespoon kosher
    mirin.
You may also use kosher teriyaki sauce instead.

2–4 cherry tomatoes
1 cabbage leaf

Cut the chicken meat into 1½-inch cubes.
Cut the leeks into pieces 1½ inches long. (If a round onion is used, cut into 4 sections
and separate each section into 2 pieces.)
Cut the green pepper into 4 sections.

Prepare 4 skewers. Fill each skewer by alternately placing chicken pieces, a piece of leek (or 1 piece of a round onion section), and 1 section of green pepper. Grill all the skewers at the same time while basting them with the soy sauce mixture at least 5 times. (If there isn't sufficient sauce, make more using the same proportions.)

Shred the cabbage leaf.

In a 7 × 4 × 2-inch box, place rice in half of the box and put *umeboshi* in the center. Cut the seaweed (*nori*) into squares and place on top of the rice in a checkerboard pattern.
Place barbecued meat and vegetables in the other half of the box; garnish with cherry tomatoes and shredded cabbage.

O-bento is a popular lunchbox carried by children to school and by husbands to the office.
The meat and vegetables, called *o-kazu*, can be tempura or any meat dish leftovers from your dinner. Rice can be mixed rice (see 8-7), green pea rice (see 8-2) or any other favorite rice.

9. NOODLES AND PASTA

Noodle dishes make an ideal lunch. In Japan, there are three ways to serve noodles. You can serve them in a large bowl with hot soup and meat and vegetables—perfect to warm you up on chilly winter days. In the hot summer, on the other hand, you can serve chilled noodles without soup and with ice cubes. You eat them with an accompanying dipping soup with meat and vegetables. Yet again, noodles can be fried and served at room temperature without soup. However you serve them, noodles make a nice lunch or casual supper.

9–1: CHICKEN NOODLES

SERVES 4

8 ounces fettuccine (or 8 ounces kosher udon noodles, e.g., Eden's udon)

12 ounces chicken meat
4 shiitake mushrooms
5 ounces frozen spinach, or 2 bunches of fresh spinach
12 snow peas
1 stalk green onion

SOUP:
6 cups chicken soup stock
2 teaspoons salt (omit if you are using ready-made soup stock with salt)
1 tablespoon sugar
2 tablespoons soy sauce
1 tablespoon white wine

Boil the fettuccine or *udon* noodles. Rinse. Drain.

Cut the chicken meat into bite-size pieces.
Slice the mushrooms.
Boil the spinach, and cut into pieces 2 inches long.
Chop the green onion.

Boil the soup stock, and cook the chicken meat in the soup for a few minutes. When the chicken is done, add all the other ingredients for the soup and then the green onion and snow peas. Boil for another minute.

Pour the boiling water over the noodles (to heat up the noodles). Drain.
Put the noodles in large individual bowls, and place the spinach on top of the noodles.
Pour the soup over the noodles.

9-2: NOODLES IN CASSEROLE (NABE-YAKI)

SERVES 4

8 ounces fettuccine (or 8 ounces kosher udon noodles, e.g., Eden's udon)

8 ounces chicken meat
8 shiitake mushrooms
2 bunches fresh spinach, or 4 ounces frozen spinach
2 stalks of green onion
4 eggs

TEMPURA:
3 ounces (12) string beans
½ Italian eggplant
½ carrot

⅓ cup cold water
⅓ cup flour
½ slightly beaten egg
dash of salt

Oil for deep-frying

SOUP:
6 cups chicken soup stock
2 teaspoons salt (omit if you are using ready-made soup stock with salt)
1 tablespoon sugar
1 tablespoon white wine
3–4 tablespoons soy sauce

Boil the fettuccine or *udon* noodles. Rinse. Drain.

Cut the chicken meat into bite-size pieces.
Slice the mushrooms.
Boil the spinach, and cut into pieces 2 inches long.
Cut the green onion into pieces 2 inches long.

162

Make the tempura topping as follows:

Trim the edges of the string beans.

Slice the eggplant and carrot thinly.

Mix all the ingredients for the batter (water, egg, flour, and salt); dip the vegetables into the batter, and deep-fry. 4 pieces of the string beans can be fried together. Drain on a paper towel.

Combine all the ingredients for the soup. Bring to a boil.

In 4 heat-resistant bowls (or small casserole bowls) distribute the noodles evenly. Place the chicken, mushrooms, spinach, green onion, raw egg, and tempura pieces on top of the noodles. Pour over the soup.

Cover the bowls, and bake in the oven for 15 minutes at 350° F. Serve in the bowls.

Note: In Japan, we cook on the stovetop using special earthenware bowls that can be set directly over a fire.

163

9-3: SESAME RAMEN

S<small>ERVES</small> 4

8 ounces egg noodles (or 8 ounces angel hair noodles)

12 ounces chicken meat

1 round onion
4 shiitake mushrooms
1 leek
2 cloves garlic
1 tablespoon sesame oil
3 tablespoons soy sauce
1 teaspoon sugar
1 tablespoon white wine

S<small>OUP</small>:
6 cups chicken soup stock
4 tablespoons soy sauce (reduce if you are using ready-made soup stock
   with salt)
1 teaspoon salt
1 teaspoon sugar
1 teaspoon vinegar
3 tablespoons sesame seeds
3 tablespoons Israeli-style tehina
1 tablespoon white wine

Boil the egg noodles. Rinse. Drain.

Cut the chicken meat into bite-size pieces.
Chop the onion and garlic. Slice the mushrooms and leek.

Heat the oil in a pan, and fry the chicken with the garlic and then the onion, mushrooms, and leek.
Add the seasoning, and fry a few more minutes.

Boil the soup stock, and add the remaining ingredients for the soup.
Pour boiling water over the noodles. Drain.
Place the noodles in 4 large individual bowls, and put the meat and vegetables on the noodles. Pour the hot soup into the bowls.

Serve hot.

9-4: DRY RAMEN (YAKI-SOBA)

Serves 4

8 ounces spaghettini (thinner pasta is better)

8 ounces chicken meat
4 cabbage leaves
1 round onion
1 carrot
4 shiitake mushrooms
2 stalks of green onion
2 ounces snow peas
2 cloves of garlic
2 tablespoons sesame oil

3 tablespoons soy sauce
1 tablespoon white wine
dash of salt

3 tablespoons vegetable oil
1 tablespoon soy sauce
dash of black pepper

Boil the spaghettini. Rinse, and drain.

Cut the meat into small pieces, and slice all the vegetables, except the snow peas.
Chop the garlic.
Heat the oil in a frying pan, and fry the garlic first and then the meat and vegetables.
Add the seasoning. Remove to a plate.

In a separate frying pan (or use the same pan after wiping clean with a paper towel), heat 2 tablespoons oil, and sauté the noodles. Add the cooked vegetables and the sauce to the noodles, and cook for 1–2 minutes, mixing well.

Serve hot with A1 sauce or table soy sauce (less salt).

9-5: FRIED RAMEN

---

12 ounces egg noodles
oil for deep-frying

8 ounces chicken meat
4 cabbage leaves
1 round onion
1 green pepper
¼ head of cauliflower
¼ head of broccoli
1 carrot
4 shiitake mushrooms
2 ounces snow peas
2 cloves garlic
2 tablespoons sesame oil

SAUCE:
1 cup chicken soup stock
3 tablespoons soy sauce
1 teaspoon salt (omit if you use an instant soup stock with salt)
1 teaspoon sugar
2 tablespoons white wine
½ teaspoon ginger powder
2 tablespoons cornstarch

Deep-fry the egg noodles for 1 minute. Drain on a paper towel.

Cut the cabbage, onion, green pepper, cauliflower, and broccoli into small pieces, and slice the carrot and mushrooms.
Chop the garlic.
Heat the sesame oil in a frying pan, and cook the meat with the garlic first and then add the vegetables.
Combine all the ingredients for the sauce, and pour into the pan. Cook until the sauce becomes thick.

Place the noodles in 4 individual dishes, and cover the noodles with the chicken and vegetable sauce.

Serve hot.

9-6: CHILLED NOODLES (ZARU-SOBA)

SERVES 4

8 ounces angel hair noodles (or 8 ounces soba noodles e.g., Eden's
*   whole-grain buckwheat pasta)*
8 ounces chicken meat
dash of salt
1 tablespoon white wine

1 tomato

2 eggs
vegetable oil spray

DIPPING SOUP:
1¾ cups chicken soup stock
⅓ cup soy sauce
¼ cup white wine
2 tablespoons sugar

2 stalks of green onion, chopped
1 sheet of seaweed (nori) cut into 2 × ¼-inch pieces

Boil the angel hair. Drain. Let cool.

Cut the chicken meat into small pieces; season with the salt and wine, and steam on a plate for about 10 minutes (see 5-2). Cut into narrow strips.

Cut the tomato lengthwise.

Spray a pan with the vegetable oil spray, and make a thin omelet with the eggs. Cut the omelet into thin 2-inch strips.

In a pan, boil all the ingredients for the soup. Let cool.

You can either divide all the food into 4 and serve individually, or serve as follows:

On a platter, arrange the noodles with ice cubes, and place in the center of the table. In a separate dish, decoratively arrange the eggs and chicken, and serve in the center of the table next to the noodles.
In 4 separate small bowls, pour the soup, and in 4 separate small dishes divide the chopped green onion and seaweed. Place them on individual place mats together with an empty plate so that diners can dip the onion and seaweed into the sauce as they eat.
Each diner will take the noodles, chicken, and eggs to his or her plate and eat by dipping in the soup with the onion and seaweed (*nori*).

9-7: CHILLED RAMEN

SERVES 4

12 ounces angel hair noodles

8 slices of smoked turkey (about 6 ounces)
½ English cucumber
2 tomatoes
3 eggs
1 sheet of seaweed (nori) cut into 2 × ¼-inch pieces

vegetable oil spray

SAUCE:
1 teaspoon salt
2 tablespoons sugar
3 tablespoons soy sauce
2 tablespoons vinegar
1 teaspoon mustard
1 cup soup stock (or water)
2 teaspoons olive oil

Boil the noodles. Rinse. Drain.
Chill the noodles in ice water.

Cut the smoked turkey into thin strips.
Cut the cucumber into thin 2-inch-long strips.
Cut the tomato into 8 sections.
Spray oil in a pan; pour slightly beaten eggs, and make a thin omelet. Cut the omelet into 2-inch strips.

Distribute the noodles evenly into 4 shallow pasta dishes.
Arrange the turkey, cucumber, tomatoes, seaweed (nori), and eggs decoratively on top of the noodles.

Combine all the ingredients for the sauce. Bring to a boil, and then cool.
Pour the sauce over the noodles, and place a few ice cubes on top of each dish.

9-8: WONTON SOUP

Dough:
1 cup flour
½ cup hot water
¼ teaspoon salt

cornstarch

Filling:
5 ounces ground meat
2 stalks of green onion
1 cabbage leaf
¼ teaspoon powdered ginger
1 teaspoon soy sauce
1 teaspoon white wine

Soup:
7 cups chicken soup stock
1 teaspoon salt (omit if you are using ready-made soup stock with salt)
1 tablespoon soy sauce
dash of powdered ginger
dash of white pepper

1 tablespoon chopped green onion

Combine all the ingredients for the dough, and knead well.

Cover with a damp cloth and leave for 20 minutes. Divide into 10 balls.

Roll each ball into thin sheets about 6 inches square on a board powdered with cornstarch. Cut each sheet into 4 small squares.

Finely chop the green onion and cabbage, and mix with the meat and the seasoning. Put a small amount of the filling (about 1 teaspoon) on a square of dough and fold diagonally. Seal tightly at the edges.

Combine all the ingredients for the soup and bring to a boil.

Drop the wonton one by one into the soup, and cook for 5–10 minutes over medium heat.

Pour the wonton soup into large individual bowls and garnish with the chopped green onion.

Note: This recipe is portioned for a meal, but if you reduce the number of wonton and the amount of soup, the recipe may be served as an appetizer.

9-9: JAPANESE PIZZA (OKONOMIYAKI)

SERVES 4

1 cup flour
1 cup cold water
1 small potato
3 teaspoons soup bouillon (powder)
4 slightly beaten eggs
2 stalks of green onion
½ round onion
4 cabbage leaves
6 ounces smoked turkey meat

4 teaspoons oil

PIZZA SAUCE:
½ cup ketchup
⅓ cup soy sauce
dash of salt
dash of black pepper
1 teaspoon sugar
1 teaspoon vinegar

Mix the flour and water.
Peel and grate the potato, and mix with the batter (flour and water).
Add the bouillon.
Add the eggs to the mixture.

Cut the green onion, round onion, cabbage leaves, and smoked turkey meat into small pieces. Combine with the batter.

Heat 1 teaspoon oil in a frying pan.
Place ¼ of the batter and vegetable mixture in the pan, forming a circular pizza about 8 inches in diameter.
Fry over a medium flame for 5 minutes, without burning. When the bottom is crispy brown, turn the pizza over. Cook the other side until browned.
Combine the ingredients for the ketchup sauce, and brush on the top of the pizza. (Reserve a portion of the sauce for the remaining pizza.)

Cook the other 3 portions in the same way.

Note: In Japan, *okonomiyaki* is cooked at the table. People go to *okonomiyaki* restaurants, where there is a large iron grill in the center of the table, and each diner cooks his or her own *okonomiyaki* pizza while chatting and drinking.

9-10: FRIED MATZO JAPANESE STYLE

4 pieces of matzo
1 large onion
1 green pepper
4 eggs
3 tablespoons soy sauce

2 tablespoons olive oil

Sour cream to top

Boil 6 cups of water in a pan. Break the matzo sheets into pieces, and soak in the boiled water for a minute or two (to soften the matzo), and drain.

Cut the onion in half, and slice it very thinly.
Cut the green pepper into thin strips.

Put all the ingredients in a large mixing bowl, and mix well.

Heat the oil (1 tablespoon at a time) in a frying pan, and sauté the mixture like a pancake.

Serve hot with sour cream.

Soy sauce is not kosher for Passover, but this is a good way to eat leftover matzo after Passover.

10. DESSERTS AND CAKES

In Japan, we usually eat fruit or cold jelly after meals. Cakes and sweets are more commonly eaten with tea in the afternoon between lunch and dinner.

Traditionally, Japanese eat sweet rice cakes with green tea. The popularity of between-meals' refreshment spread with Zen Buddhism in medieval times. The sweet cakes eaten during tea ceremonies usually are not homemade but are professionally prepared goods bought at shops.

In this chapter, I introduce some jelly and fruit desserts that can be made at home.

10-1: JELLY COCKTAIL WITH DATE PASTE

SERVES 4

DATE PASTE:
8 ounces seedless dates
½ cup chopped walnuts
¼ cup orange juice
1 tablespoon orange peel

JELLY:
2 tablespoons kosher agar (or unflavored kosher gelatin to firm 2 cups water)
2 cups cold water
½ cup sugar

FRUITS:
1 banana
1 pear

SYRUP:
½ cup (8 tablespoons) maple syrup

Date paste:
In a food processor, combine all the ingredients and process until they form a paste. Knead well, and form into balls. Place to the side.

Makes about 1½ cups paste. You can use the leftover paste for other desserts, such as milk jelly and jelly cocktail.

Jelly:
Soak the agar in the cold water for 20 minutes, and gradually bring it to a boil (or dissolve the gelatin in hot water) and add the sugar.
Pour in a square mold and chill.

Dice the gelatin, and place the cubes into 4 small glass bowls. Pour 2 tablespoons maple syrup over the gelatin cubes in each bowl.

Fruits:
Slice the banana and cut the pear into small pieces, and arrange over the agar/gelatin cubes. (You can use any of your favorite fruits.)
Top with the date paste.

Serve chilled.

10-2: JELLY COCKTAIL

JELLY:
2 tablespoons kosher agar (or unflavored kosher gelatin for 2 cups water)
2 cups cold water
½ cup sugar

SYRUP:
½ cup (8 tablespoons) maple syrup

FRUITS:
2 slices of pineapple
1 banana
3 halves of canned apricots (or canned peaches, or 2 fresh peaches)
4 scoops of vanilla ice cream (optional)

Soak the agar in the cold water for 20 minutes, and gradually bring to a boil (or dissolve the gelatin in hot water) and add the sugar.
Pour in a square mold and chill.
Dice the gelatin, and place the cubes into 4 small glass bowls. Pour 2 tablespoons maple syrup over the gelatin cubes in each bowl.

Cut all the fruits into small pieces, and arrange over the agar/gelatin cubes.
Optional: Top with the ice cream.

Serve chilled.

10-3: DATE JELLY (YOKAN)

S ERVES 4

10 ounces seedless dates
¼ cup Sabra liqueur (or sweet wine)
¼ cup water
2 tablespoons agar (or unflavored kosher gelatin to firm 2 cups water)
2 cups cold water
2 tablespoons honey
1 tablespoon lemon juice

Soak the dates in the liqueur and water overnight.

Grind in a food processor.

Soak the agar in the cold water. Leave for 20 minutes, then bring to a boil, stirring constantly (or dissolve the gelatin in hot water) and add the sugar.

Add the honey and the dates to the gelatin, and cook for 5–7 minutes over a medium flame, stirring constantly.

Let cool. Add the lemon juice. Pour in a small mold, and chill in the refrigerator.

To serve, cut into slices.

10-4: SNOW JELLY

SERVES 4

5 tablespoons agar (or unflavored kosher gelatin to firm 5 cups water)
2 cups sugar
5 cups cold water

4 egg whites
2 tablespoons sugar
Fruits in season

Soak the agar in cold water for 20 minutes; add the sugar, then bring to a boil (or dissolve the gelatin and sugar in 5 cups water while beating steadily). Let cool a little.

Beat the egg whites until stiff, and add 2 tablespoons sugar. Just before the gelatin begins to set, slowly add the egg whites, stirring constantly. Let set firmly in the refrigerator.

Decorate with sliced fruit, using colorful fruits to provide contrast to the white jelly.

10-5: MILK JELLY

---

3 tablespoons agar (or unflavored gelatin to firm 3 cups water)
1 cup cold water
⅓ cup sugar
2 cups milk

4 tablespoons maple syrup

Soak the agar in the cold water for 20 minutes, and bring to boil (or dissolve the unflavored gelatin in the hot water).

Add the sugar and milk. Cool in the refrigerator for a few hours until the jelly becomes firm.

Dice the milk jelly.

Place the jelly into 4 individual bowls; pour 1 tablespoon maple syrup.

Serve cold.

10-6: ORANGE JELLY

SERVES 4

4 oranges
2 tablespoons agar (or 1 packet of unflavored kosher gelatin, or 1
    packet of orange-flavored instant jelly)

2 cups orange juice
¼ cup sugar

Cut the oranges in half; remove the orange flesh from the rind with a grapefruit spoon.
Place the flesh into the 8 orange rinds.
Soak the agar in the orange juice for 20 minutes, and bring to a boil (or dissolve the
unflavored gelatin in the juice). Add the sugar.
Pour the mixture into the 8 orange rinds, and chill in the refrigerator.

10-7: SPONGE CAKE (KASUTERA)

SERVES 4

5 eggs
⅔ cup sugar
¼ cup honey
¾ cup flour

Preheat oven to 325° F.
Grease and flour a baking dish 8 inches square and 4 inches deep, or an equivalent-sized loaf pan.

Separate the eggs.
Beat the egg whites until stiff, and gradually add the sugar.
Beat the egg yolks, and mix with the honey.
Fold the egg yolk mixture into the egg whites, and beat until thick.
Sift the flour, and mix lightly with the eggs.
Pour the batter into the pan, and bake for 40 minutes.

The cake is cut into 1-inch pieces and eaten without frosting, accompanied by tea or coffee. This Western-style cake was introduced by the Portuguese who arrived in Nagasaki in the sixteenth century.

10-8: FRIED APPLE

SERVES 4

2 apples

BATTER:
1 cup flour
1 slightly beaten egg
⅔ cup cold water

Oil for deep-frying

½ cup maple syrup

Peel the apples and remove the cores. Cut each apple into 8 sections.

Put the flour in a bowl, and gradually stir in the water and egg to make a smooth batter.

Heat the oil.
Dip the apples in the batter, and deep-fry. Drain on a paper towel.

Pour the syrup.
Serve warm.

Note: You may substitute 4 bananas cut into halves.

10-9: GRAPES IN JELLY

S ERVES 4

15 kyoho (or large) grapes
3 cups Kedem sparkling chardonnay grape juice (or any good-quality,
  natural 100% grape juice with no sugar added)
3 tablespoons agar

Peel the grapes.

In a pan, pour the grape juice, and add the agar. Leave for 20 minutes.

Bring the juice to a boil, stirring constantly, and simmer for 5 minutes until the agar is dissolved.

Pour into a loaf pan. Cool to room temperature.

Put the peeled grapes in the jelly one by one.

Chill in the refrigerator.

When the jelly becomes firm, remove from the loaf pan, and slice into ½-inch pieces.

APPENDIX

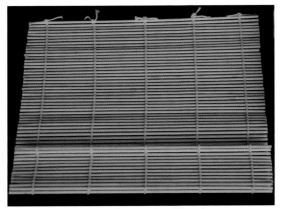

A sushi roller made of bamboo.

Parch (or toast) sesame seeds and crush them.

Making Japanese food kosher is easier than you think.